DANCE

Tibetan
dance mask

Ballet tutu

Bharata
natya
dancer

Nigerian
dance staff

Headdress for
ballet dancer

Javanese ear
and arm
ornaments

Costume
designs

Dancing
bodhisattva

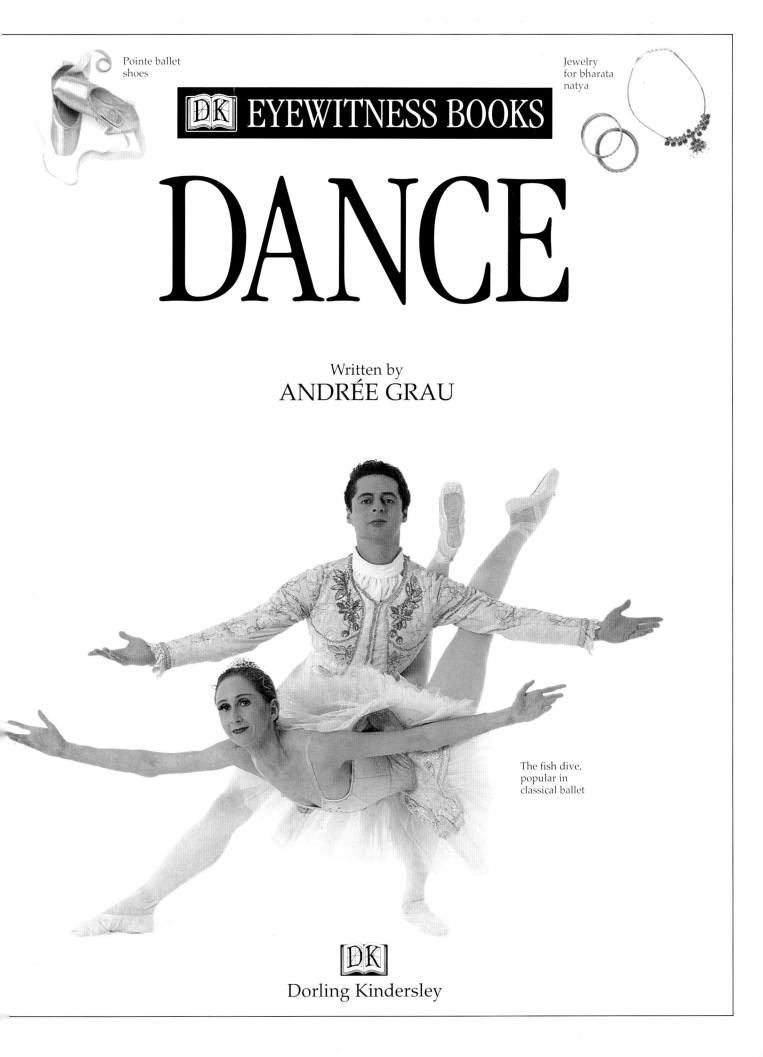

Pointe ballet shoes

Jewelry for bharata natya

DK EYEWITNESS BOOKS

DANCE

Written by
ANDRÉE GRAU

The fish dive, popular in classical ballet

DK

Dorling Kindersley

Pointe ballet
shoes

Finger cymbals,
Morocco

Court dancer,
Java, Indonesia

Dorling Kindersley
LONDON, NEW YORK, DELHI, JOHANNESBURG, MUNICH, PARIS and SYDNEY

For a full catalog, visit
 www.dk.com

Project editors Cynthia O'Neill and Marian Broderick
Art editor Cheryl Telfer
Picture research Louise Thomas
Senior managing editor Linda Martin
Senior managing art editor Julia Harris
Production Lisa Moss
DTP designer Nicky Studdart
Special photography Andy Crawford

This Eyewitness ® Book has been conceived by
Dorling Kindersley Limited and Editions Gallimard

© 1998 Dorling Kindersley Limited
This edition © 2000 Dorling Kindersley Limited
First American edition, 1998

Published in the United States by Dorling Kindersley Publishing, Inc.
95 Madison Avenue, New York, NY 10016
2 4 6 8 10 9 7 5 3 1

Dorling Kindersley books are available at special discounts for bulk purchases for sales promotions
or premiums. Special editions, including personalized covers, excerpts of existing guides, and
corporate imprints can be created in large quantities for specific needs. For more information,
contact Special Markets Dept., Dorling Kindersley Publishing, Inc., 95 Madison Ave.,
New York, NY 10016; Fax: (800) 600-9098

Library of Congress Cataloging-in-Publication Data
Grau, Andrée.
Dance / written by Andrée Grau.
p. cm. (Eyewitness Books) Includes index.
Summary: Surveys all forms of dance throughout the world,
discussing its cultural and social significance, its costume,
its history, and noted dancers and choreographers.
1. Dance — Juvenile literature.
2. Dance — Cross-cultural studies — Juvenile literature.
3. Folk dancing — Juvenile literature.
[1. Dance.] I. Title.
GV 1596.5.G73 2000   792.8 — DC21
98–17269
ISBN 0-7894-5877-2 (pb)
ISBN 0-7894-5876-4 (hc)

Color reproduction by Colourscan, Singapore
Printed in China by Toppan Printing Co. (Shenzhen) Ltd.

Metal anklet,
Ghana

Thigh bell,
Kenya

Jazz dancer, USA

Contents

Kathkali dancer, India

What is dance?

DANCE IS A SERIES OF MOVEMENTS performed in patterns and set to an accompaniment. Every human society practices dance, which may be performed solo, in couples, or in groups. People around the world use dance to express themselves, pass on their histories, and exercise their bodies. In this way, dance can be a celebration of the emotional, mental, and physical human self. It can also be a preparation for battle or an unspoken protest. Dance is often used to mark major life changes or to commemorate an important event in a nation's history. In the earliest societies, dance helped humans survive – it was a way for communities to learn cooperation in working and hunting together – and, like today, dance was probably used to communicate and express feelings that are difficult to convey in any other way.

Dinka folk dancer, Sudan, Africa

Steps of difficult folk dances take time to master

JOY OF DANCE
When experiencing great joy, we often feel an urge to leap and dance. For many people, Gene Kelly's exuberant dancing in the film *Singin' in the Rain* (1952) is a perfect illustration of the joy of dance.

LOST DANCES
Dances, unlike many other works of art, are not fixed in time – they exist only while being performed. Many dances, such as the galliard of the 16th century, are no longer performed, and the moves are now lost. An early engraving gives us only the faintest idea of what the galliard might have looked like.

DANCES AS A FOLK FORM
Certain dances are created by and belong to particular groups of people and are passed down through generations. In many parts of Africa, these dances can reinforce a people's sense of identity, or can be used to celebrate rituals or rites of passage.

DANCE AS AN ART FORM
Modern dance has generally been against the classical forms, such as ballet. However, some contemporary dancers have retained the visual poetry of classical dance – both European and African – while mixing it with impulsive gestures from folk and street dance, creating a new art form.

Briefly held statuelike poses come from the classical tradition

Classical leg shapes of ballet

Modern hand movements

An "isolation," in which one body part moves independently of the others

A graceful improvisation from folk or street dances

Eye contact adds to the sensuality of the tango

Body shapes are perfectly symmetrical

Clothing is chosen to emphasize the swirling fluidity of jazz dance movements

BANNED DANCES

Some dances are disapproved of so much by society that they are banned. In 1913, German army and navy personnel could be dismissed for dancing the tango. In 1956, during one of Elvis Presley's first television appearances, cameras showed him only from the waist up, because the gyrating movements of his hips were considered shocking.

ORDER AND RHYTHM

In ancient Greece, dance was seen as the gift of the immortals. The Greek word, *chora,* meaning "source of joy," resembles *choros,* the Greek word for "dance." Order and rhythm, the main qualities of dance, were also the qualities of the gods. The philosopher Plato wrote that dance "gave the body its just proportions."

Buddhist dancing figure, China

SACRED DANCES

Many religions, such as Buddhism and Hinduism, use dance as a part of worship, and dancing figures are often seen in shrines of these faiths. Other religions have ritual gestures instead of dance – special movements performed by priests while reading from sacred texts, or special postures adopted while praying. In medieval times, walking the maze of Chartres Cathedral in France was part of religious worship.

Foot moves echo those of ballet

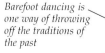

Barefoot dancing is one way of throwing off the traditions of the past

Learning to dance

WE ALL LEARN to dance in our own way, whether by imitation or instruction. Different societies have different ideals for a dancer's body. Some dancers, including Southeast Asian classical dancers, are expected to have a particular look. Every day they practice exercises that develop their muscles and posture in specific ways, creating extraordinary dancers' bodies. Other dance styles accept a variety of body shapes and sizes, but all require great stamina and flexibility. In some places, dances are only for young people, and performers retire when they reach middle age, or even before. Other societies appreciate that dancers acquire more depth in their style as they grow older.

For practice, Cambodian dancers wear comfortable clothes, but are literally sewn into their costumes in performance

Thumb and index finger create a classic offering gesture

CLASSICAL CAMBODIAN DANCE
A slow, almost hypnotic pace, and smooth wavelike movements characterize the classical dance of Cambodia. To achieve the effect, dancers need to develop a high degree of articulation, or flexibility, in all their joints. Students practice special exercises that make their fingers and elbows so supple that they appear to be without bones.

A walking step

Flexibility of the ankle joint is important, as it helps dancers move in a gliding fashion

A cyclic pattern that twists and spirals, from the center of the body

MARTHA GRAHAM
For Martha Graham (1894–1991), there was nothing more wonderful than the human body. She saw dance as a celebration of the miracle of the body's beauty, and she called dancers "athletes of God." Like athletes, her dancers were expected to move in a disciplined way and to carry out a daily regime of exercises based on her principles of contraction, release, and spiral. Graham's dances were designed to reveal a person's inner landscape – what she called the "cave of the heart."

The Song, choreographed by Martha Graham, 1985

DOING THE SAMBA, BRAZIL
The samba is a fast-moving dance that, like many South American dances, has African and Caribbean roots. In preparation for Rio de Janeiro's annual carnival, dancers practice for months in samba schools – neighborhood social clubs whose main purpose is to organize carnival processions. A prize is awarded every year to the best samba school, and competition is fierce.

Graham's dances incorporated a lot of floor work

LEARNING TO DANCE IN BALI

In Bali, Indonesia, dance lessons tend to be public occasions where everyone is free to watch. The Balinese are interested not only in dance performance but in the entire learning process. Children learn dance forms mainly through imitation (known as nuwutin), but dance teachers also manipulate the limbs of their young students by placing them in the correct positions. Even before a child begins formal instruction – maybe even before he or she can walk – relatives bend the child's arms and hands into the correct positions.

Balinese children learn to achieve a tranquil, masklike facial expression

A quiet intensity and alert eyes characterize most Balinese dance

Stylized and graceful dance, such as that of Japan, suits older dancers

Symmetry is usually an important part of Japanese dance

Arms are held at sharp angles

The gracefulness of arm and hand movements are a major part of Balinese dance

OLD AND YOUNG

Dance is not the prerogative of the young – in Asia, for example, older dancers are admired. Both youthful and elderly Japanese celebrate the coming of spring once a year by dancing at sakura festivals. With the cherry blossom trees spectacularly full of bloom, the dancers honor the beauty and short lifespan of their national flower.

Torso is held straight with a slightly arched spine and the shoulders slightly up

Limbo pole is lowered after each successful attempt, to add a competitive element

Fire makes the dance even more of a display – and even more competitive

Brightly colored material is made into a sarong and wrapped around the dancer

LIMBO DANCING

Many folk dances have a competitive element. During carnivals and other celebrations in the Caribbean, young dancers often show off and compete with each other by performing dances that include acrobatic feats. One of these, known as the limbo dance, originated in West Africa. While it looks spontaneous, it actually requires a suppleness and agility that is built up over an extended period.

Balinese dance is performed barefoot

11

Ballet class

Each variety of dance is made up of techniques that need to be mastered by its dancers. These techniques have been refined, sometimes over hundreds of years, to create an ideal of beauty. To achieve this ideal, some dancers dedicate their lives to dance, learning their skills through discipline and years of training, beginning in childhood. For example, in classical ballet, dancers have to be elegant, long-limbed, and straight-backed. They need amazing stamina and every movement must appear effortless. Ballet dancers, no matter how exalted their positions in the company, attend class daily to keep their bodies in peak condition and to maintain control over their muscles and movements.

BUILDING STRENGTH
To make difficult lifts look effortless, male dancers must be strong. Along with studying the steps, boys train using special exercises that build their strength without making their physiques too bulky. These exercises are strictly supervised.

Exercises to strengthen the upper body are important for male dancers

SCHOOLS AND COMPANIES
Prestigious ballet companies are often affiliated with ballet schools. Many dancers with the world-famous Kirov Ballet (above) began at the Kirov School in St. Petersburg, Russia.

Dance pupils at the Royal Ballet School in London

Dancers learn basic moves correctly at the barre

Back is straight

Knees bent over toes

Thighs horizontal to floor

1 BEGINNER'S EXERCISES
Among the first movements a beginner learns are pliés (bends) and relevés (raises). These "easy" moves must be practiced many times to get them right. This is the starting position for a grand plié in second.

2 Pliés help to stretch and strengthen a dancer's leg muscles. The dancer bends smoothly and slowly into a demi-plié (half bend), with his feet turned out and his heels on the floor.

3 The dancer bends further, into a grand plié (full bend), keeping his heels on the floor. He takes care to keep his movements controlled and smooth throughout.

LEARNING ARABESQUES

As dance pupils progress, they move on to more difficult movements, such as the arabesque. In this beautiful position, a dancer balances on one leg with her other leg extended behind her and makes a long, slanted line with her body. Dancers are taught the basic kinds of arabesque first, such as the low arabesque, shown at right.

The upper back is kept straight

Head is kept up

Front hand is turned palm down, following the line of the arm

A diagonal line is created by the left leg and the right arm

DEGAS AND THE BALLET

More than half the paintings by the French Impressionist painter Edgar Degas (1834–1917) feature young ballerinas. In his richly colored work, the artist captured behind-the-scenes moments, such as this ballet class. The elderly teacher, leaning on his stick is, in fact, the choreographer Jules Perrot (1810–1894), who earlier in his career choreographed the romantic ballet *Giselle*.

LIFTING HIGHER

As a dancer builds up strength, she is able to lift her leg higher behind her. Her body makes a beautifully curved line from her raised foot to her shoulder, and she is perfectly balanced. Her arms stretch out softly in flowing harmony with her body.

Working leg

ADVANCED ARABESQUES

A pupil who has studied ballet for years can perform more advanced movements such as the move shown at right. The dancer balances on demi-pointe. She turns her head to look over her front shoulder. In this expressive movement, the dancer can raise and lower her working leg in a sweeping motion.

Soft, flowing line

Dancers hold the barre for support during certain exercises

In a demi-pointe, the dancer stands on the ball of her foot

Legs appear to be crossed to the audience

BALLET STUDIOS

Mirrors line the walls of dance studios so that pupils can check their positions during class. The wooden floor is specially constructed to "give" slightly when dancers land from a jump. This protects their joints from uncomfortable jarring. A wooden handrail, known as a barre, runs around the wall.

ARABESQUE CROISÉ À TERRE

There is a great variety of arabesques, and ballet pupils learn how each can express different moods and feelings. In the arabesque known as croisé à terre, the dancer's back and neck make a graceful line. The dancer concentrates on maintaining the correct placing of her legs and holding her hips level.

Accompaniment

Dance usually combines movements with music – but not always. Sometimes dance can be accompanied by other, nonmusical sounds, such as street noise, insect or animal sounds, or even the rhythmic banging of a door. Dance can also be accompanied by meaningful texts, such as beautiful or sacred poetry. It can even be performed in silence. The relationship between dance and its accompaniment varies widely, but musical or otherwise, accompaniment is vital to establishing the right atmosphere. In European and American dance theater, for example, the orchestra is usually hidden from the audience, whereas in other parts of the world, the musicians are often on display and greatly contribute to the visual spectacle.

Drumsticks can be hit together to create another percussion sound

TONGA DANCE
Traditional sung poetry, often based on myths and legends, accompanies some dances on the Pacific island of Tonga. The dancer interprets important words in the poem. For example, if the text mentions a flower, the dance may represent a breeze carrying the flower's fragrance. The dances are usually performed standing or sitting, and include graceful hand and arm movements.

CLAPPING AND THE CUECA
In the cueca, a Chilean dance for couples, guitars provide the main accompaniment, but singers and dancers punctuate the music with handclaps. This lively dance and accompaniment inspired the song "America" in Leonard Bernstein's hit musical *West Side Story.*

DRUMMING IN AFRICA
Because Africa is a large continent with more than 50 countries, there is an immense variety of dance music, ranging from unaccompanied traditional singing to the "talking" drums of West Africa, which imitate the sounds of speech. Drum music is also especially popular in Burundi and other parts of East Africa. The drums used in large ensembles, such as the one below, have to be tuned carefully because the melody is as important as the rhythm they provide.

Drum ensembles usually have a leader

Drums are tuned by tightening the wooden screws

Animal hide stretched over tree trunk

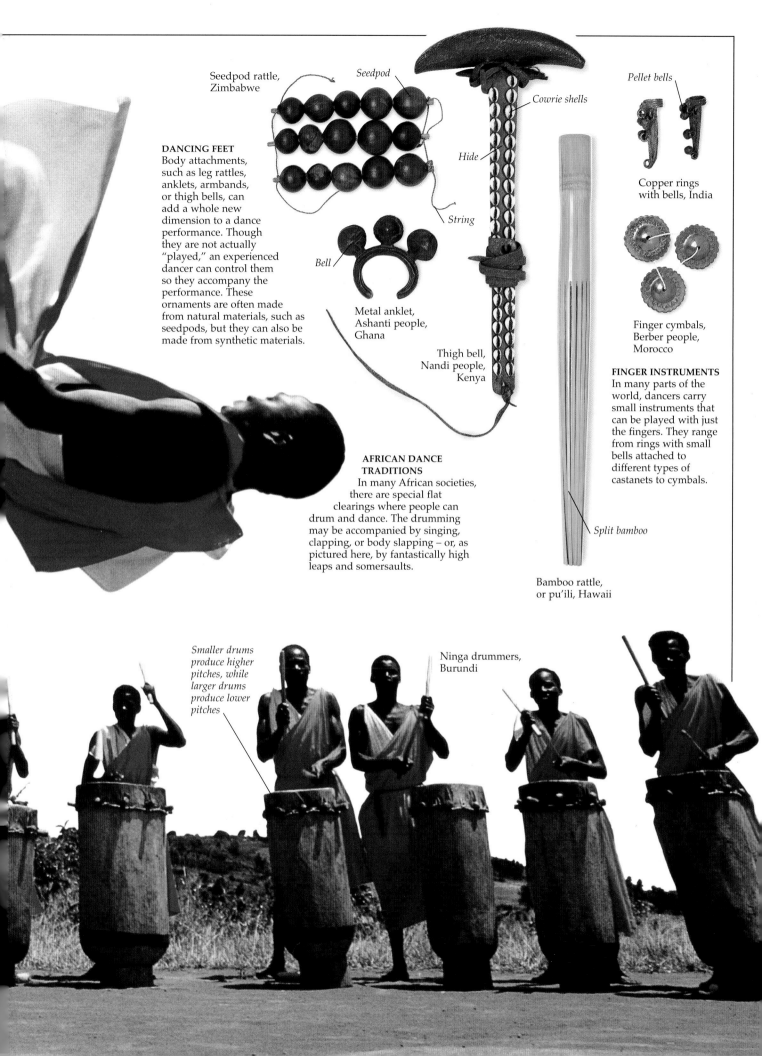

Seedpod rattle,
Zimbabwe

Seedpod

Cowrie shells

Hide

Pellet bells

DANCING FEET
Body attachments,
such as leg rattles,
anklets, armbands,
or thigh bells, can
add a whole new
dimension to a dance
performance. Though
they are not actually
"played," an experienced
dancer can control them
so they accompany the
performance. These
ornaments are often made
from natural materials, such as
seedpods, but they can also be
made from synthetic materials.

String

Bell

Copper rings
with bells, India

Metal anklet,
Ashanti people,
Ghana

Thigh bell,
Nandi people,
Kenya

Finger cymbals,
Berber people,
Morocco

FINGER INSTRUMENTS
In many parts of the
world, dancers carry
small instruments that
can be played with just
the fingers. They range
from rings with small
bells attached to
different types of
castanets to cymbals.

**AFRICAN DANCE
TRADITIONS**
In many African societies,
there are special flat
clearings where people can
drum and dance. The drumming
may be accompanied by singing,
clapping, or body slapping – or, as
pictured here, by fantastically high
leaps and somersaults.

Split bamboo

Bamboo rattle,
or pu'ili, Hawaii

*Smaller drums
produce higher
pitches, while
larger drums
produce lower
pitches*

Ninga drummers,
Burundi

Keeping time

We all have a sense of ourselves and of other people moving through space and time. In dancers, this sense is highly developed. Dancers are aware of their bodies and of the effect of their movements on an audience. When they are carrying out one action, they are mentally anticipating the next; they subtly adjust the movements leading to the next step, in order to prepare the audience. Performers use rhythm to establish this kind of exchange with an audience. Rhythm is a timing system that develops on a basic pattern of silences and pauses. Performers cannot ignore the laws of rhythm, and cannot dance without a sense of rhythm, but they can carve out their own ways of interpreting it. Whether it is the fast, exciting rhythms of the Spanish flamenco, or the slow, controlled rhythms of Japanese nō, successful dancers create their own timing on top of a basic rhythmic pattern.

TIWI PEOPLE, AUSTRALIA
Among the Tiwi Aboriginal people of Melville and Bathurst islands, clear lines and rhythm are essential for movements to be considered dance. These performers specialize in "strong dancing," where every change must occur exactly on the beat. Movements flowing across the rhythm exist in the Tiwi repertoire, but they are performed only as song gestures.

Sumptuous costumes are made of gold and silver brocade

Masks used in nō are an art form in themselves

NŌ DANCERS
The Japanese dance-drama nō is a majestic and beautiful art form. The gestures, breathing, and music in each scene of each performance are underlined by the complex idea of *Jo-ha-kyu*, which concerns the rhythmic relationship between two forces, pulling in opposite directions. Nō is very slow-moving, and performances are extremely long. It has been compared to watching a flower change imperceptibly and eventually shed its petals.

Nō relies on symbolism, often provided by props

Kathak dancers occasionally dance in pairs

KATHAK
In Indian music, rhythm is expressed by tal, a system of beats that gives a dance its structure. The dancers of kathak, an energetic dance form from northern India, are expert at improvising intricate steps with their feet while making graceful movements with their arms. Kathak dancers are involved in a "conversation" with musicians, which develops as the performance goes on. They explore the cycle of beats individually, but at key moments of the music cycle they synchronize their timing.

The Four Temperaments, 1946

FOUR TEMPERAMENTS
Listening to some music, George Balanchine (1904–1983) was moved "to try to make visible not only the rhythm, melody, and harmony but even the timbres [tones] of the instruments." In 1946, he set a ballet to Paul Hindemith's *The Four Temperaments* that tried to represent, through pure dance, what was in the composer's mind musically.

Elegant arm and hand movements of flamenco are sometimes reinforced with the use of a fan

A scene from *Choreartium* (1933)

FLAMENCO
The origins of the flamboyant Spanish dance known as flamenco are obscure. Some say flamenco originated in the southern province of Andalusia. Others say it came to Andalusia with gypsies, who traveled from India and Pakistan via Egypt and that the roots of flamenco are in the kathak. In both flamenco and kathak, sophisticated footwork creates rhythmic patterns and the dance itself acts as percussion. Improvisation may still be practiced, and dialogue with the musicians is crucial in both.

Performers manipulate their costumes as part of the dance

SYMPHONIC BALLET
In the 1930s, the Russian choreographer Léonide Massine created a number of ballets set to symphonies. *Choreartium*, which was set to Brahms' Fourth Symphony, was his second. Although other choreographers had previously arranged ballets to symphonies, they were isolated productions. Debate raged around Massine's work – some people felt that dancing to symphonic music somehow debased the symphony.

Castanets are not a traditional part of flamenco but are used in the folk dances of southern Spain

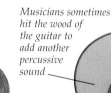

Musicians sometimes hit the wood of the guitar to add another percussive sound

FLAMENCO AND ACCOMPANIMENT
The three main components in flamenco are singing (cante), dancing (baile), and guitar (guitarra). Performances originally included only singing and dancing, with some handclapping (toque de palmas). The guitar came later, first as accompaniment, then as a solo instrument in its own right.

Special shoes have nails driven into the soles and heels are used to add percussion

Themes and messages

DANCE DOES NOT ALWAYS SIMPLY tell a story. It may be used to bring people together, by reinforcing their shared beliefs about their place in the world or celebrating their relationship with the supernatural. Some dances, such as the Native American ghost dance, were created to channel frustration and bring hope for the future. Others, such as the haka of New Zealand, are war dances that can raise aggression against enemies. Some communal African dances teach the young the values of society by showing the path they are expected to follow. In contrast, other dances, such as modern antiwar ballets, challenge society's values and inspire new ideas.

Club represents the owner's supernatural helper

Arapaho ghost dance club, 1800s

GHOST DANCE
This dance was a response by the Native Americans of the Great Plains to intolerable poverty and oppression. Carrying carved clubs, they danced in appeal to their gods to restore traditional ways and bring back the buffalo. The dance was banned by the white authorities.

BUFFALO DANCE
The buffalo dance, as shown in this 19th-century painting, carries a message of respect for the animals that are about to be killed. Tribes such as the Blackfoot promised the buffalo that life taken from it in this world would be returned in the next. They believed that a sacred ritual dance had the power to make this happen.

Buffalo heads worn during the dance

Dancers entered a hypnotic state

DANCING AGAINST WAR
With his ballet *The Green Table* (1932), Kurt Jooss tried to move people to take action against the evil political system of fascism, which was overtaking Europe in the 1930s. The ballet is about the two-faced nature of some diplomats, and how they must shoulder the responsibility for the deaths caused by war.

Kurt Jooss

Masks worn by the dancers

Shouting and warlike gestures accompany the haka

Traditional wooden weapons are used as part of the haka

DANCING FOR WAR
Throughout the world, dance has been used to drill warriors, both to strengthen their muscles in preparation for hand-to-hand combat and to unify the fighters. The Maori people of New Zealand traditionally performed a war dance known as the haka before battle and in victory celebrations afterward. Today, New Zealand rugby teams prepare for their matches in world competitions by performing the haka before kickoff.

GREAT DOMBA SONG

Among the Venda of South Africa, young women prepare for marriage and integration into adult life by learning the milayos – the laws set out in poems and riddles – and dancing the domba. The domba requires extremely good timing and cooperation.

HARVESTS AND CROPS

Dances are performed at harvest festivals around the world to celebrate the end of a successful farming year. The ritual is thought to help regenerate the earth in preparation for the next harvest. Such dances also promote social unity and cooperation in the face of the dangers and whims of nature.

Ankle or shin bells add to the rhythm of the dance

The colors blue and yellow represent a town called Letchworth in the heart of England

Fresh flowers adorn hats to represent spring and regeneration

MORRIS COSTUME

Morris dancers emphasize group unity by dressing alike. They wear white shirts, flowered straw hats, and ornamental sashes known as baldrics. Morris costume sometimes includes bells attached to the shin that ring in time with the movements of the dance.

MORRIS DANCE

Traditionally performed at local festivals in the South Midlands of England, morris dancing is performed today throughout the country. It was once an exclusively male ceremonial dance but now is danced by amateurs of both sexes – often in competitions. Categories of the dances include processional, jig, and set dancing. Team dancing is deliberately boisterous – this reinforces team spirit amongthe participants, especially in competition.

Sticks or handkerchiefs are often used

Baldrics

Team colors

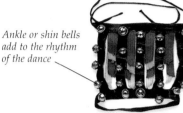

Telling tales

DANCE TELLS STORIES in many ways. Some dances use mime, facial expressions, and movements that have specific meanings. For example, kathakali performers in southern India use a code of gesture that literally translates the text sung by an accompanying vocalist. Often, however, dance uses stories that are already well-known. Western audiences know the story of *Sleeping Beauty* from childhood, while Indian children are taught the many mischievous adventures of the god Krishna, his ways with milkmaids, and his love for the beautiful Rhada. In every society, people watch dance because it has the power to bring a special interpretation to these popular tales. The very deepest human emotions – love, betrayal, despair – can all be expressed in dance.

Firebird is dressed in red

This move is designed to indicate struggle – the prince is forcing the firebird to help him

FIGHT BETWEEN GOOD AND EVIL
Ballet stories are often about love winning against cruelty and malice. In *The Firebird* (1910), a magical bird of fire helps Prince Ivan rescue a beautiful princess and rid the world of an evil magician known as Kostchei.

BURMESE PUPPET
In the puppet theaters of Southeast Asia, well-known stories are told by Burmese marionettes, like the one above, Indonesian shadow puppets, and Vietnamese water puppets.

Iconic gesture of flute playing always represents the god Krishna

Lion face

Fish

ELOQUENT HANDS
Hand gestures in bharata natya are known as hasta or mudras. Some hand gestures are iconic – they look like what they represent. Others are symbolic – they are abstract gestures.

BHARATA NATYA
The classical Indian dance form bharata natya blends two very different but complementary types of movements: expressive dance, which interprets classical poetry through mime, and abstract dance with rhythmic improvisation. Hand gestures and stylized facial expressions (abhinaya) are crucial.

Prince Albrecht wooing Giselle

Giselle plucking a daisy

STORY OF *GISELLE*
The ballet *Giselle* (1841) tells of a simple village girl overwhelmed by the attention of Albrecht, a prince disguised as a peasant. When Giselle discovers that Albrecht has deceived her and is already engaged, she kills herself with his sword and joins the Wilis, the spirits of young girls betrayed in love. In Act I, Giselle's symbolic movements, such as playing he-loves-me, he-loves-me-not with a flower, emphasize her innocence.

EXPRESSING EMOTION THROUGH DANCE
A pas de deux in ballet is a dance for two
performers, usually a man and a woman. It
presents a relationship – often a beautiful vision
of romantic love – from its first awakening to
the great joy of its realization. The dancing of a
pas de deux can be intimate, or extravagant and
full of passion. Between sections of dancing
together, each performer traditionally performs
a solo dance, known as a variation, showing his
and her individuality.

*Ornate, romantic
costumes create
the right mood
for a love story*

*Male dancers
always look at
the ballerina*

*This arabesque
penché (bent forward)
is one of the most
beautiful expressions
of romantic love*

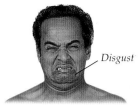

Disgust

Valor

KATHAKALI
Performers of this
Indian dance develop
phenomenal control over
their facial muscles, eyes,
and lower and upper
eyelids. Through stylized
facial expressions, a huge
range of emotions, such
as valor, revulsion, love,
anger, compassion,
derision, wonder, and
fear can be conveyed
to the audience.

*Dancers train
from childhood
to achieve great
strength yet
softness in
the hands*

*Serene expression
is part of the
choreography*

*Strong knees
and thighs are
essential for
supporting
and lifting*

CELESTIAL NYMPH
Thai dancers, like
Indian dancers,
tell of the heroic
mythological beings
from the *Ramayana*,
an ancient epic
poem. However,
unlike the Indian
hasta, Thai hand
gestures do not tell
the story literally,
but are designed to
add beauty and
grace to the overall
shape of a dance.

*Fingers, palms,
and wrists
contribute to
the overall shape
of the dance*

Beauty and strength

PEOPLE EVERYWHERE TAKE PLEASURE in beautiful objects, music, and dance. Yet what is seen as graceful or lovely in one culture can be thought ugly or inappropriate in another. For example, it is shocking for a traditional Indonesian audience to see a ballerina extend her legs, because in Indonesian dance women do not display their legs in this way. Around the world, there are many different sets of rules that decide "good" and "bad" taste. All the members of a community share these rules – but occasionally artists bend or disregard them to introduce new ideas and overcome boundaries.

JAVANESE COURT DANCER, INDONESIA
At the sultan's court on the Indonesian island of Java, there is a pure dance style called bedoya, which is performed only by women. The Javanese court dancer must seem to move smoothly and effortlessly. Her graceful, rolling movements are thought to represent the spiritual refinement and wisdom of kingship.

Gilt-edged sampur

Gentle angles or slow movements convey the serenity and elegance of the dance

ROYAL RWANDANS
The royal Tutsi dancers of Rwanda reenact past heroic deeds. This dance commemorates the courageous defense of the kingdom from cattle raiders. The dancers try to represent the vigor and nobility of an ideal warrior. The dancers are accompanied by the royal drums, and symbolize the king's authority.

Legs are kept hidden in Indonesian dance

Hair ornament

Ear ornament

ADORNMENTS
Javanese dancers wear delicate jewelry and accessories, such as ear ornaments made from gilded buffalo hide. Their dancing also contains stylized gestures such as playing with earrings or adjusting a head ornament.

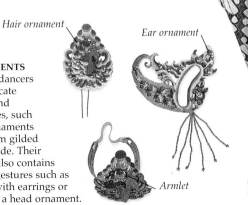

Armlet

FLOWING WATER
Female classical dancers on Java embody the Javanese ideals of beauty, proper behavior, and spiritual growth. In both dance and life, Javanese custom has it that a woman's movements should be quiet, restrained, and modest – and as calming as flowing water. This dancer gently waves her sampur, or scarf, to emphasize the grace and flow of her movements.

Feet are kept close together and stay in contact with the floor

The higher the leap, the more prestige the Cossack dancer gains

COSSACK LEAPS
In many cultures, only men perform high jumps. Russian soldiers known as Cossacks, for example, use their vital dance style to show off their agility, physical prowess, and technical skills. The Cossacks like to compete for prestige by outdoing each other's acrobatic feats.

MALE DANCER, JAVA, INDONESIA
Unlike female dancers, whose feet scarcely lose contact with the floor, Javanese male dancers – usually depicting warriors – execute wide, sweeping movements and postures. Similarly, while the focus for a female dancer's eyes is generally limited to the floor for a distance of two to five steps, the forceful male dancer can extend the focus of his eyes forward to a distance three times his height.

The design of these gilded ear ornaments is of Hindu origin

The heroes of one popular dance-drama, the Ramayana, *are usually portrayed as archers*

This angular Javanese stance is based on an ancient Indian posture

Leg lifted so that thigh is parallel with the floor

Heroic dance often features traditional weapons, such as a sword, as part of the costume

Brown is one of the most popular colors used in Javanese costume

HIGHLAND LEAPS
While some dance forms are "earthed," almost caressing the ground, others use high leaps that seem to defy gravity. Scottish Highland dance emphasizes both elevation and swift foot movements, which contrast sharply with the stiffness of the upper body.

Hands are together in a gesture of reverence

Sharp angles created by arms

CREATING A WARRIOR
This Javanese dancer achieves a regal and martial posture by straightening his body, forcing his wrists and elbows into sharp angles, and creating another wide angle with his knee. In contrast to Western ballet's extended foot, Javanese dancers tense the toes upward.

Wide leg gestures are acceptable for male dancers

Weight-bearing leg is kept straight

Foot and knee must be turned out sideways

Fancy footwear

MOST DANCE STYLES are about the way dancers use their feet. Whether shaped by special shoes or left free, dancers' feet determine their basic postures and movements of a dance. The development of ballet shoes shows how footwear and dance styles influence each other. Until the 1810s, ballerinas wore simple slippers and kept the balls of theirfeet in contact with the floor. However, audiences wanted ballerinas to seem as light as air, and this led to dancing en pointe (on the tip of the toes). To dance this way, ballerinas relied on specially constructed reinforced shoes.

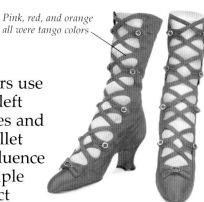

Pink, red, and orange all were tango colors

TANGO BOOTS, 1910s
When the tango craze hit Europe in the early 20th century, dancers opted for boots in hot "tango colors."

TIPPYTOES
Since its invention in the 1810s, dancing en pointe has been identified with classical ballet techniques.

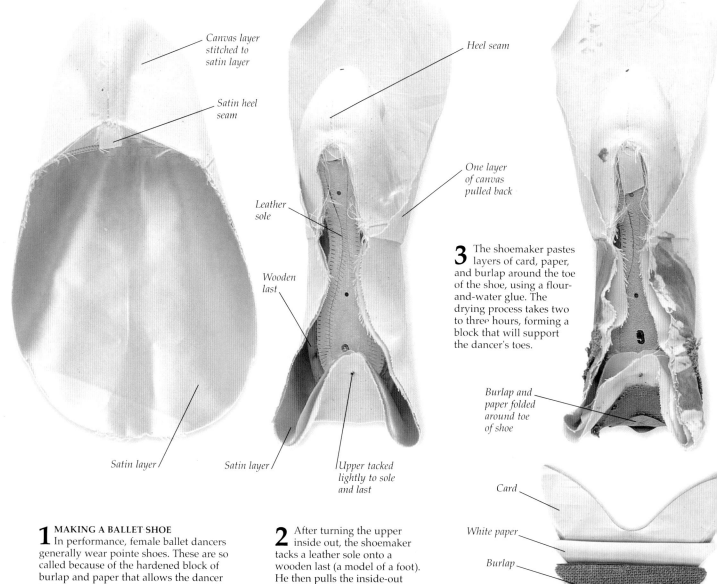

Canvas layer stitched to satin layer

Satin heel seam

Heel seam

One layer of canvas pulled back

Leather sole

Wooden last

Satin layer

Satin layer

Upper tacked lightly to sole and last

3 The shoemaker pastes layers of card, paper, and burlap around the toe of the shoe, using a flour-and-water glue. The drying process takes two to three hours, forming a block that will support the dancer's toes.

Burlap and paper folded around toe of shoe

Card

White paper

Burlap

Different thicknesses of gray paper

1 MAKING A BALLET SHOE
In performance, female ballet dancers generally wear pointe shoes. These are so called because of the hardened block of burlap and paper that allows the dancer to dance en pointe. Despite the delicate appearance of the satin upper, these shoes are quite stiff. The shoemaker begins the shoe by stitching together satin and canvas layers to make the upper.

2 After turning the upper inside out, the shoemaker tacks a leather sole onto a wooden last (a model of a foot). He then pulls the inside-out upper onto the last and peels back one layer of canvas. The shoemaker tacks the upper to the last, through the leather sole.

Ankle bells accompany the dancer as she stamps her feet

Designs painted on with henna emphasize the curved lines of the feet

Platform soles decorated with rhinestones

PAINTED FEET
In bharata natya, a classical Indian dance style, performers decorate their feet instead of wearing shoes. The designs complement the patterns painted on their hands.

PLATFORM SOLES
Performers in traditional dance forms such as Japanese kabuki and Chinese opera wear shoes with elevated soles. Platforms have also been popular in more informal contexts, such as the disco fashions of the 1970s.

STILT DANCERS
In areas of southern and western Africa, dancers perform on stilts up to six feet (two meters) high. Leg-crossing, jumps, and twirls are precarious, but that is partly the point of the stilt dance. Finding the right balance symbolizes the wisdom of humankind.

Stilt dancer, Ivory Coast

Heel

Shoe turned right side out

Leather insole

Drawstring

Sole is stitched to upper

Layer of canvas is pulled forward to cover the paper-and-glue block

Wax thread

Canvas is stitched in tight pleats around the block

Shoemaker's mark

Dancers soften new shoes to shape them to their feet – some soften shoes by closing them in a door!

Satin ribbons, normally about 1 in (2.5 cm) wide and 1.5 ft (50 cm) long

4 When the glue has dried, the peeled-back layer of canvas is pulled forward and pleated around the toe with metal pincers. The shoemaker stitches the hard leather sole to the upper, using wax thread. The shoe is removed from the last and turned the right way out. A leather insole is then inserted before the shoe is put back on the last.

5 The shoemaker shapes and fashions the shoe with a special smooth hammer. This tool is also used to shape the pointe into a platform. Finally, the finished shoes are put into a warm oven to harden for 12 to 15 hours.

6 Traditionally, dancers sew the ribbons onto their own shoes and often embroider the toe area to stop the fabric from fraying. Pointe shoes have a remarkably short life; principal dancers in a ballet company wear out about a dozen pairs a month!

Makeup

THROUGHOUT THE WORLD, performers apply makeup to dramatize their features. Whether they use ochers, charcoal, synthetic materials, or paints made from powdered stones, makeup has many uses. It highlights beauty; transforms humans into heroes, demons, or animals; or acts as a mask, hiding a dancer's identity. In India, kathakali performers use makeup to transform themselves into mythical beings. In Africa, Woodabe men use makeup and dance to express their inner beauty.

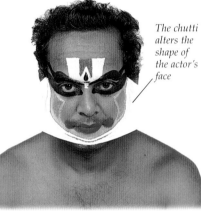

Traditional makeup is applied with an erkila, a stick made from a stripped coconut leaf

1 APPLYING KATHAKALI MAKEUP
In kathakali, a dance-drama from South India, an artist applies layers of makeup. The colorful and elaborate designs, which take up to four hours to complete, have been handed down over centuries.

CHINESE OPERA
In Chinese opera, makeup defines characters and covers the actor's whole face. Until early in the 20th century, men performed all the roles – even that of beautiful princesses!

Eyebrows are strongly defined, as they are an essential element of beauty

A princess is made up in white, red, and shades of pink

The chutti alters the shape of the actor's face

"STILL LIFE" AT THE PENGUIN CAFÉ
The stunning costumes and makeup used in the modern ballet *"Still Life" at the Penguin Café* helped to reinforce its ecological message about endangered species.

2 ATTACHING THE CHUTTI
One of the most distinctive aspects of kathakali makeup is the chutti – a white "frame" that focuses the audience's attention on the actor's face. Traditionally, the makeup artist constructs the chutti from specially cut paper and inserts it into layers of rice paste. Applying the chutti takes at least an hour.

Dancers dust their faces with yellow powder

A special seed, the chundapoo, is washed, cut, and inserted into the eyelid to make the eyes look bloodshot

BEAUTY CONTESTS FOR MEN
The Woodabe people of Niger, West Africa, hold dancing competitions so the women can decide which man is the most attractive. A contestant uses makeup to emphasize his eyes, his long, thin nose, and his white teeth, and he uses facial expressions to show off his inner beauty.

DRESSING ROOM
Backstage at the ballet, dancers make themselves up in dressing rooms assigned according to rank: the more important the dancer, the bigger the dressing room. The corps de ballet share a space, but principal dancers have their own rooms and often their own makeup artists.

3 MAKING THE EYES RED
When the chutti is dry, the actor applies the rest of his makeup. As a final touch, he cuts a seed known as a chundapoo and inserts it into his eyelid. The cut seed dyes the white of the eye red, and this highlights the expressive eye movements that are a major part of a kathakali performance.

The heavy kiritam (headdress) is made of wood and inlaid with imitation gemstones

SPECTACLE OF KATHAKALI

Kathakali narrates the heroic adventures from India's two most famous epics, the *Mahabharata* and the *Ramayana*. Dealing with the constant struggle between good and evil, kathakali is highly spectacular and often involves a fierce battle that results in the destruction of a supernatural demon. The ornaments, movements, and especially the costumes and makeup emphasize the sacred nature of the characters. Noble-hearted heroes always have green faces, while actors playing treacherous schemers paint their faces dark red or black.

Coconut shell, holding rice paste

Spirit gum

Erkila

Chutti coil

Paper to make chutti

Paints

COLORS AND TOOLS

Rocks are ground up and mixed with coconut oil to produce the vivid paints used by kathakali actors. Spirit gum and then rice paste are applied with a chutti coil to paste the chutti paper to the actor's face.

The kiritam is usually painted in red, green, white, and gold

The eyebrows and eyes are exaggerated with black makeup

ABORIGINAL DREAMING

In central Australia, Aboriginal dancers apply ocher and soft feathers to their bodies in geometrical designs. The designs and makeup have great religious importance, linking the dancers to their ancestor spirits and to the Dreamtime – the time of Creation.

Costumes in dance

DANCE COSTUMES ENHANCE A PERFORMANCE in a wide variety of ways. For example, in traditions where there are no stage sets, costumes help the audience make sense of the action. Costumes often follow specific codes; for example, the size of a headdress or the length of a sleeve may say something about the character. Costumes can be stunning in themselves, but their impact is usually reinforced with makeup, music, and gesture. This combination immediately helps an audience tell the loyal from the treacherous, the good from the wicked, and the admirable from the despicable. Costumes can veil, obstruct, round out, or emphasize the contour of the dancers' bodies and movements. They add a whole new dimension to dance.

Warriors often wear long pheasant feathers in their headdress

Nō kimono, Japan

Graceful movements of the pheasant feathers are part of the dancer's gestures

CHINESE OPERA
In Chinese opera, warriors are important characters. They bring visual excitement with their acrobatic moves. Both male (wusheng) and female (wudan) warriors wear costumes that allow for ease of movement. Trousers enable the dancers to perform spectacular high kicks.

Opaque tights highlight the beautiful line of the leg

Modern transparent material

ALL-IN-ONE COSTUMES
Choreographers of western contemporary dance, such as Maurice Béjart of France, focus on the expressive power of movement. The all-in-one costume used in his work *Malraux* (1986) allows the spectators to see all the movements of the choreography.

HISTORICAL COSTUME
Costumes can indicate historical periods without being exact historical replicas. In Yolande Snaith's *Gorgeous Creatures*, the main character is recognizably Queen Elizabeth I of England. While her clothing is inspired by the period, it is made of modern material that allows for interesting dance movements

NŌ DRAMA, JAPAN
The kimono (left), worn in nō, transforms the proportions of the performer's body. The wide sleeves create a contrast between the overall pyramid shape and the narrowness of the wrists. In performance, a belt is placed well above the waist.

PAVLOVA'S DYING SWAN
Michel Fokine's *La mort du cygne* (1905) became associated with Anna Pavlova just as, generations before, the name of Marie Taglioni conjured up a vision of *La Sylphide*. It is rumored that Pavlova's last words were about the dance and that she died clutching her costume (right).

Real swan feathers made the costume realistic

Colorful, hand-embroidered motifs

GEORGIAN BALLET
Dancers of the Republic of Georgia wear very long costumes that hide their feet. When they move they seem to glide across the floor as if mounted on wheels, and the audience cannot see how the effect is achieved.

Light, flowing material

Headdress size and design is determined by role

Red jacket symbolizes a heroic role, while demons wear black and Lord Krishna wears dark blue

Skirt is supported by many layers of cotton underskirts

KATHAKALI COSTUME
Kathakali performers wear extremely ornate clothing. The color of the jacket depends on the character; the jacket is open at the back so that the performer can be cooled by fanning. The vast skirt is made up of many layers of white cotton, with a decorated top layer. The performer varies the skirt's length by splaying his knees and legs.

Outside of the foot bears the weight

Masquerade costume, Nigeria

IBO MASQUERADE COSTUME
Masquerade costumes hide the identity of the performer. Often padding is sewn in to exaggerate or create additional body parts. This costume is worn by the Ibo men of Nigeria, West Africa, who imitate young girls as part of the annual harvest celebrations. Traditionally, a mask completes the masquerade outfit.

Costume design

Cᴏꜱᴛᴜᴍᴇꜱ ᴀʀᴇ ᴀɴ ɪᴍᴘᴏʀᴛᴀɴᴛ part of dance. In some traditions they act as a moving set – against a bare backdrop, they help place the characters in context. Costumes may complement or enlarge the movements of the dancers. In Chinese classical dance, performers wear long sleeves, which they manipulate to create beautiful shapes, while in Javanese classical dance and Spanish flamenco, female dancers kick back their trains. Some costumes have ancient origins: in India, the costumes of modern classical dancers are based on temple sculptures. Since costumes are a traditional element of most dances, they are not often redesigned for particular performances. However, they are usually adapted to make the most of modern technology: it is more convenient to use Velcro than hooks as fasteners. In western theater dance, however, innovation is highly valued as part of the dance experience, and dance costumes are regularly redesigned.

Vividly colored stripes resemble sunrise

Short-sleeved coat

CHINESE CONJUROR
The Chinese conjuror (sorcerer) is one of the characters in *Parade* (1917), a ballet that satirizes a troupe of entertainers. Picasso's sketches for the magician's costume are outlandish, matching the tone of the ballet.

PICASSO'S DESIGNS
Pablo Picasso (1881–1973), one of the greatest artists of the 20th century, designed costumes for the ballet. From 1917, he worked with the Ballets Russes in Paris. Many of his first costumes for the ballet *Parade* were influenced by cubism, a style of modern art that Picasso founded. The costumes created a small sensation.

Early costume designs for a prima ballerina

Rich but somber colors hint at melancholy theme of ballet

Sample costume fabrics

1 DESIGNING FOR THE BALLET
At the start of the design process, the artistic director briefs the costume designer on the production. For example, the ballet might have a melancholy atmosphere in Act III, and the costumes need to reflect this. The designer then sketches early ideas. With some ballets, certain traditions must be observed: in a classical ballet, such as *Sleeping Beauty*, lead ballerinas always wear short costumes known as tutus. With newer ballets, designers can be more flexible.

Paper patterns for costume

2 MAKING THE COSTUME
The designer sketches ideas for every costume that will appear in the ballet. Once the director approves these ideas, the designer turns them into patterns – guides for cutting the fabric, usually made of paper or cardboard. The costume is then sewn, with alterations being made after it has been fitted to the dancer.

Headdress of twisted gold echoes details of lace on cloak

Motif of vine leaves and grapes

Synthetic pearls form clusters of grapes

ALL IN THE DETAIL
In major ballet productions, even the costumes for lesser characters are designed with great detail. The Cavalier of the Golden Vine is a minor character in the ballet *Sleeping Beauty.* Nonetheless, this costume from a 1946 production is lovingly embroidered, even though it would be almost impossible to see the details from the auditorium!

Cloak is removed and hung up to become part of the set

4 USES FOR COSTUME
When Eurydice first appears to Orpheus, she is weighed down with a heavy cloak. Since it is obviously uncomfortable for a dancer to perform in a heavy costume, the costume is designed so that the ballerina can remove the cloak after the initial impact of its appearance.

3 INTO THE UNDERWORLD
When Adonais Ballet Company decided to put on the new ballet *Orpheus,* costumes were commissioned that would reflect the story. The ballet is based on the Greek myth of the musician Orpheus, who is overcome with grief when his new wife Eurydice is killed, and descends to the dark shadows of the underworld to find her. Eurydice's costume is designed to show that she is now a spirit, trapped in this gloomy realm.

5 PERFORMANCE
The dancer now performs in a leotard and chiffon wrap. The wispy drapes still suggest the spirit world, but do not weigh the dancer down. The costume shows off her technique; here, the chiffon highlights the beautiful shape of the arabesque.

Behind a mask

A DANCER'S FACE is one of the most expressive parts of the body, yet there are dances all over the world in which performers prefer to use masks to cover their faces. By concealing themselves behind masks, performers can let go of their own identities and devote themselves completely to the movements. Wearing masks challenges dancers to use their bodies in particular ways, so that every part becomes more expressive. In addition, masks can have a symbolic meaning: they may represent spirits or gods, dead ancestors, or the prized skills of a highly respected animal. Wearing a mask allows a performer to take on the special qualities of someone – or something – else.

LITTLE OLD MEN DANCE MASKS, MEXICO
Clownlike figures are part of many mask traditions. In the Mexican state of Michoacán, wooden masks painted pink represent the *viejito*, or little old man, a grandfather cavorting around in a humorous manner.

WAR DANCE, PAPUA NEW GUINEA
Men performing a war dance wear frightening masks, carry weapons, and cover their bodies with mud. Their dance represents the eternal battle between good and evil, light and darkness.

Carved skulls add to the drama of the dance

Mask is lavishly gilded with gold leaf

Papier-mâché is molded and then painted

TIBETAN MOUNTAIN DANCERS
In the Himalaya Mountains, dancers wear wooden masks painted in bright colors (left). The performers, moving in slow rhythm in time to deep-sounding drums, dance both on festive occasions and at times of ill fortune. Masks like this represent the spirits of their mountain gods.

Boldly colored geometric designs

IBAN DAYAK, SARAWAK, BORNEO
The Iban Dayak, Sarawak's largest native group, traditionally use painted wooden masks (left) at harvest festivals, when dancers celebrate the end of the harvest and the fertility of the land. These dances also celebrate the connection between Iban Dayak society and the cycle of the natural world.

FÊTE DE MASQUES, IVORY COAST
West African countries are famous for their mask dances. Masks are usually worn to conceal the identity of the performer. The Ivory Coast has a festival of masks every year.

Bar supplies leverage to pull open the beak

Mask has a dual purpose: to represent the eagle and to reveal the human

RANGDA MASK, BALI, INDONESIA
According to Hindu tradition, wives were killed when their husbands died. In Balinese dance, the unpopular rangda, or widow figure, represents women that survived. The witchlike rangda possesses dangerous magical powers – only the strongest performer can withstand her spirit.

Rangda is depicted as shaggy and wild

Drawstring pulls the mask aside to reveal the human face beneath

Rangda has fangs and a long, hanging tongue to devour children

KWAKIUTL
Among the Kwakiutl of the American Northwest, traditional priest-doctors called shamans often wear masks during ceremonies. These connect the shamans with the powers of their ancestors. The masks often represent admired creatures, such as the eagle depicted here.

COURT DANCE, THAILAND
In Thai court dances, beautifully ornate papier-mâché masks, featuring an elaborate golden top, are worn by male dancers to celebrate special occasions such as the king's birthday. Although Thailand is a Buddhist country, court dances usually depict one of the great Hindu epics. One such story, the *Ramayana,* relates the heroic deeds of the god Vishnu in his disguise as Rama, the king of Ayodhya.

Realistic costumes and masks

ANIMAL MASKS
For a ballet based on the tales of Beatrix Potter, costumes and masks – neatly arranged in the Royal Ballet's storeroom when not in use – re-created each animal character in minute detail. Although the masks and costumes were inhibiting, the dancers transmitted the personality of each character – such as the delightful Squirrel Nutkin, pictured above – through their movements, which were brilliantly choreographed by the British dancer and choreographer Frederick Ashton (1904–1988).

Dance and worship

DANCE BRINGS TOGETHER thoughts and feelings, and can create special, deeply felt emotions. In some areas of the world, such as Australia, India, Africa, and parts of western Asia, certain dances are linked to religion and are regarded as sacred: to those dancers, dancing is a form of prayer. Even in places where dance is not connected with worship, dancers say that the experience can be transcendental – in other words, it is a way to leave everyday life behind and climb into the realm of the spirit.

Expressive eyes and hands are most important

AN ANCIENT ART
In India, practically all performing arts have close links with religion. Bharata natya is linked to ancient temple dances in Tamil Nadu, southern India. The dancers came from special families and were known as devadasis.

This dance movement closely resembles one of the popular postures of Siva, the Indian lord of the dance

DEVADASIS IN THE COMMUNITY
In traditional Indian society, secular and religious activities were not clearly separated. Devadasis and their dances were important for rituals such as weddings, as well as for entertainment in royal courts.

WHIRLING DERVISHES
The dervishes are Muslim friars, originally from Turkey. When dancing, they spin around faster and faster with their arms spread out until eventually they enter a trancelike state. In this higher state of mind, they believe it is possible to be in contact with God.

Pleats are practical as well as beautiful

Necklace

Anklets add percussion to the moves

Anklet

Hair ornament

DANCING TO REACH THE DREAMTIME
In Australia, Aboriginal people dance as a way of reaching a timeless zone they call the Dreamtime. According to ancient belief, this was when the universe and everything in it was created. Dancing the sacred dances re-creates the universe and helps keep everything in its proper order.

COSTUME AND JEWELRY
When bharata natya was reconstructed in the 1930s, the costume was based on temple sculptures and everyday life. Most Hindu statues are adorned with jewelry, so this became part of the look. Since devadasis used to be dedicated to the temple god by being symbolically married to him, the costume has become popular with brides.

Ornaments and jewelry resemble those of a bride in Tamil Nadu, India

MOVING THROUGH SPACE
When performing in a confined space, bharata natya dancers suggest space through the use of their body and particularly their eyes, rather than through large movements across a floor.

BHARATA NATYA TODAY

Today, bharata natya is performed in theaters as a solo concert dance. The modern art form combines elements of mood, music, and drama. The term comes from joining together parts of the words *Bhava* (emotion), *Raga* (melody), *Tala* (rhythm), and *Natya* (drama). The expressiveness of the dancer, rather than her pure athletic ability, is bharata natya's most important quality. Although dancers are no longer married to the gods, bharata natya is often based on stories of gods, goddesses, and heavenly nymphs, and a performance always begins and ends with a dedication to God.

Jewelry and flowers make the dancer resemble Hindu statues

Ogun, the god of iron, blacksmiths, and war

DANCE STAFF, NIGERIA

The Yoruba of Nigeria use iron dance staffs to mark the distinctive rhythms for dances associated with individual gods. Each staff is connected to a particular god.

Circle of fire

Hand shapes and movements are precise

Medieval bronze of Siva Nataraja

LORD OF THE DANCE

Siva Nataraja, the Indian lord of the dance, is just one aspect of the great Hindu god Siva. The four-armed Siva Nataraja is always shown dancing. He represents the creation-death-regeneration cycle of the universe.

A demon crushed by Siva

RUTH ST. DENIS

Ruth St. Denis (1877–1968), one of the pioneers of American modern dance, sought to celebrate the spiritual in her dances. She looked for inspiration in mythologies from around the world, and she created many exotic dances based on her idea of what she called "the Orient." Though these dances were immensely popular, they were far from authentic.

Pleats fan out to reinforce the shape of the dance

Court dance and pageantry

SPECIAL DANCES, known as court dances, have been used throughout history to represent the ruling powers. All over the world, these ruling powers have also made sumptuous and spectacular pageants a part of court life. These great spectacles displayed both their wealth and their control over vast numbers of people. Special court dances – regal and measured in their movements and performed on significant national occasions, for example – reinforced the sense that a king is somehow different from his people and strengthened the position of a ruler. Court dances tend to be different from other dances. They are hierarchical, setting those at the source of power apart from the ordinary folk. Court dances have had far-reaching effects – they have given rise to the classical forms of dance in Europe, Asia, and Africa.

Bugaku performers were traditionally male but were made up to perform female roles

Kimonos used for bugaku are splendidly decorated

Mask represents Matsubara, a dragon king

Mask is made of wood, lacquer, and human hair

BUGAKU COURT DANCE
The bugaku and gagaku of Japan represent the world's oldest unbroken tradition of court dance and music. Some of today's performers claim they are 39th generation – that members of their family have performed these dances and music throughout the last 1,200 years! Some dances depict legendary battles, while others tell the story of meetings with supernatural beings and mythical beasts. The costume for bugaku often includes spectacular face masks.

Long, full kimonos are used for the more serious bugaku, which are known as "left" dances

A NATIONAL TREASURE
Bugaku is a dance of great dignity and stateliness in which the performers move very slowly and elegantly in simple symmetrical patterns. For centuries, only the imperial household, government officials, and their guests were allowed to enjoy bugaku – the public could watch only after World War II. Today, these court dances are seen as reflecting qualities in the Japanese national character, and in 1995, bugaku and gagaku performers were proclaimed "living national treasures."

OCTOBER 1 PARADE, BEIJING, CHINA
In China, one of the major celebrations is the National Day festival on October 1, which commemorates the day in 1949 that the Communist Party swept to power after years of revolution and established the People's Republic of China. A love of pageantry and display comes to the fore at festivals such as this, with colorful and perfectly synchronized fan dances such as the one performed above.

The striking of stately poses is central to bugaku

COURT DANCE, GHANA
Carried by his courtiers, the elected king of the Ashanti in Ghana makes an impressive entrance. On special occasions, the king dances before his people to display his royal virtues. His dance movements are powerful but slow and dignified. The royal umbrella shading the king is also made to "dance" in time to the drums.

Ashanti finger rings, made of gold and encrusted with jewels

Golden Ashanti daggers

ASHANTI GOLD
Arab travelers in the 8th century described Ghana as "the land of gold," and for centuries gold has been the Ashanti people's emblem. Even today the king may dance while weighed down with masses of gold jewelry and ornaments. In the past, the golden heads of heroic Ashanti kings decorated the royal throne, and a gold stool symbolized the unity of the nation.

SUN EMBLEM
History remembers Louis XIV of France as *le roi soleil* – the Sun King. In 1653, at age 15, Louis performed as the rising sun in *Le ballet de la nuit*. In 1654, he performed as Apollo, the Greek sun god, in *Les noces de Pelée et de Thétis*. His costumes were liberally decorated with images of the sun.

Costume features emblems representing the sun

DANCE AT THE COURT OF LOUIS XIV
During his reign, Louis XIV drew the aristocracy to Versailles, his court outside Paris. The king was a well-known lover of dance; to be invited to dance in his presence was an honor that could launch a career, and Louis himself often performed. There was, however, an ulterior motive to Louis' court dances. By forcing the aristocrats to spend lavishly to keep up with his extravagance while also keeping them away from their bases of power in the provinces, Louis kept them under his control financially and politically.

Louis XIV as the rising sun, Le ballet de la nuit, 1653

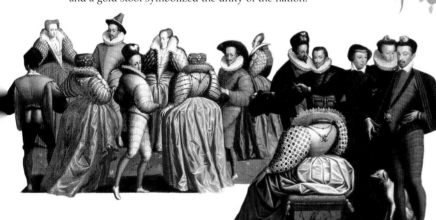

EUROPEAN COURT DANCE
In the 16th century, European princes competed with each other to have the most sumptuous court, emptying their treasuries to stage extravagant spectacles. In 1581, Catherine de' Medici and her son Henri III organized a royal wedding that included a series of court balls. These balls, held at the Louvre in Paris, were so lavish that they set the standard for all subsequent celebrations.

National heritage

PEOPLE DANCING TOGETHER share a sense of belonging. Dancing can remind them of their cultural identity and give them a sense of pride in their heritage. This experience can be particularly important in times of hardship, poverty, or oppression. When people find themselves powerless within their own country because it has been colonized, or when they have had to migrate because of economic difficulties or war, dance can return to them a sense of self-worth. Dance reinforces a sense of community and gives the outside world a positive image of a valuable heritage. Indeed, throughout history, there are examples of traditional dance being revived just as the first moves toward independence are made. Often this process polishes and standardizes the dances.

The dragon king always includes the traditionally lucky colors of bright yellow or gold

The dragon is formed of up to 12 sections, 3–9 ft (1–3 m) in length

DRAGON DANCE
In Chinese mythology, the heavenly dragon represents prowess, nobility, and good fortune. Traditionally the dragon dance was used to expel devils and bring people good luck. It was an essential part of many celebrations. Today it is especially associated with the Chinese New Year and is performed throughout the world wherever large Chinese communities have settled. The dragon is followed by a noisy procession filled with drumming, fireworks, and cheering crowds.

Several dancers, one drummer, and one leader are needed for the dragon dance

Chinese dragon dance

DANCING FOR INDEPENDENCE
Until the 19th century, the sardana of Catalonia, northeast Spain, was a simple dance, confined to a small area and performed by few people. As the Catalans unsuccessfully fought for independence from Spain, the dance spread, and became a symbol of Catalan rebellion. During the 20th century, the fascist Franco government tried unsuccessfully to ban the sardana.

QUETZAL DANCE, MEXICO

In an effort to rediscover their preconquest identity, native Mexicans organized themselves into dance associations. At festivals and all-night vigils they perform traditional Aztec dances – some of which are named after Aztec gods, including the most powerful god of all, Quetzalcoatl.

Pheasant feathers

Quetzalcoatl, the fabulous Aztec plumed serpent god of light

Headdress

Back of an Irish dance costume

Irish symbol of the shamrock

ORISSI, EASTERN INDIA

The classical Indian dance orissi was at one time performed only by temple dancers called mahari. Like other classical forms, it was the subject of a cultural revival from 1930 to 1950, just as serious moves toward independence from Great Britain were being made.

Orissi dancer

Green, white, and gold were favorite colors

Irish rose of handmade lace

Ute chief in tribal dress

IRISH DANCE AND IDENTITY

At the turn of the century, traditional Irish dance changed from an informal pastime into a symbol of nationalism. Dances were standardized, and costumes became highly decorative. They were often adorned with Celtic designs copied from a 9th-century illuminated manuscript, the *Book of Kells*, which had just been discovered. Irish dance helped create an image of Irish nationhood.

Kikuyu dancers performing a courtship dance

Soft dance shoes

NATIVE AMERICAN POWWOW

White Americans frowned upon large intertribal gatherings, or powwows, because they felt threatened. In the 1930s, as Native Americans feared the loss of their cultural identity, they turned powwows into dance competitions, in which the dances of a glorious native past could be passed down to younger generations.

Soft shoes allowed for intricate movements in dances, such as the slip jig

KIKUYU DANCERS, KENYA

In many East African societies young couples traditionally perform courtship dances. These dancers are performing such a dance for tourists, using adapted traditional movements.

Role reversal

WOMEN MAY DANCE AS MEN, and men as women, for a number of reasons. For example, in France in the late 19th century, ballet dancing had become a female activity, and women took over the male roles. The male lead in *Coppelia* (1870) was choreographed for a ballerina called Eugénie Fiocre. In 17th- and 18th-century China and Japan, it was considered improper for women to go on stage, so some male performers began to specialize in female roles. Role reversal is often thought of as humorous. All over the world, there are pantomimes featuring men dressed as women – the humor lies in the fact that the performers are obviously male and wear outrageous costumes. On the other hand, the Venda people of South Africa use role reversal in dance for a serious reason – it helps confuse evil spirits who might otherwise harm the dancers. Today in dance, the more common role reversal involves a male dancer playing a female role.

GROTESQUE FEMALE ROLES
In romantic ballet, female dancers represent the essence of beauty and elegance. There is a convention in ballet that such beauty cannot perform ugly roles, so these roles are performed by men dressed as women. In Frederick Ashton's *La fille mal gardée* (1960), Lise, the daughter of Widow Simone, loves Colas, but her mother is determined to marry her to Alain, the feeble-minded heir of a rich farmer. The ballet is full of slapstick and comic effects, both in the characters and in the choreography.

SALOME BY BÉJART
Only 10 lines are devoted to Salome in the Bible, yet her story has been portrayed and elaborated in all the arts, especially dance. Invited to dance at court in celebration of Herod's birthday, Salome pleased the king so much that she was allowed to ask for whatever she wanted. Her mother advised her to demand John the Baptist's head. Salome has usually been portrayed as a sensual woman, but the French choreographer Maurice Béjart wanted to break the stereotype of the female seductress and cast a man in the role.

Widow Simone, a caricature of a woman played by a man, here resembles a pantomime dame

CARABOSSE IN *SLEEPING BEAUTY*

The evil fairy Carabosse in *Sleeping Beauty* (1890), the Ugly Sisters in *Cinderella* (1948), and Widow Simone in *La fille mal gardée* (1960) are all comic or grotesque female roles played by men. In *Sleeping Beauty*, Carabosse places a curse on a baby princess. The curse is meant to kill her, but a good fairy, Lilac, changes it so that it makes the princess and her family sleep for 100 years.

Carabosse (right) in *Sleeping Beauty*

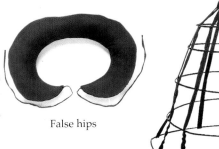

False hips

Crinoline

CARABOSSE'S COSTUME

The role of the reclusive Carabosse is traditionally danced by a man. As the evil fairy moves menacingly around the stage, her earthy, wicked nature is often depicted by a costume that enlarges her body with false hips and a crinoline. Over these Carabosse wears a dress of dusty, ragged black.

SWAN LAKE, ADVENTURES IN MOTION PICTURES

Matthew Bourne's version of *Swan Lake*, choreographed in 1995, stunned audiences. The ballet features no dainty ballerinas. Instead, the swans are bare-chested men in feathery pantaloons, who convey both birdlike grace and a ferocity unknown in more traditional versions. They represent the assertive and masculine side of the male lead, Prince Siegfried, instead of the feminine grace and elegance of the lead ballerina, Odette/Odile.

KABUKI ONNAGATA

In many Japanese classical dance forms, only men were allowed to perform publicly. Since plays contained female roles as well as male, some actors specialized in these. In the traditional dance form known as kabuki, these specialists are called onnagata, which means woman-person. Elaborate makeup and costume help transform a mature man into a beautiful young woman, but the main transformation takes place in the gestures, bearing, and voice of the performer. Kabuki actors are trained not only to move like women on stage but also to think like women.

An onnagata headdress is often extremely ornate

Costumes can weigh up to 40 lb (18 kg) and are lavishly decorated

Kabuki kimonos are designed so they can be removed to transform the dancer into another character

41

Something old, something new

DANCE LINKS PAST and present, ancient and modern. For dance to be properly appreciated, it needs to create images that are understood by its audience: if a dance is too remote, people will not be able to make sense of it. Dancers use the traditions of the past in various ways and for a number of reasons. Some reject tradition because they feel it is not relevant to the present – they want to create dances that address contemporary issues. Others feel that they want to rediscover a golden, more meaningful past. Yet others see their work as the logical development of a thriving tradition.

ANCIENT TRADITIONS
From the time they were rediscovered, the painted and carved images of ancient Greek dancers have inspired modern dancers, including Isadora Duncan, who have admired and emulated their elegance.

LOOKING FOR INSPIRATION
The American dancer Isadora Duncan (1878–1927) is the figure most noted for loosening the restrictions of ballet, which she considered unnatural and damaging. In her search for the real source of dance, she turned first to the art of classical Greece, second to nature, and third to herself. She once claimed her style of dance was "the art lost for two thousand years."

Duncan's clothing and costume were also inspired by ancient Greece

Motifs found on Greek friezes adorned the fabric of Duncan's costumes

Wildflowers are often embroidered in bright colors on folk costumes for both men and women

COPPELIA
In the ballet *Coppelia* (1870), a young man named Franz becomes so smitten with the charm of a mysterious "girl" that he forgets his fiancée, Swanilda. The girl, however, is nothing but a doll. The dancers' costumes are inspired by a romantic idea of what central European peasantry might once have worn. Swanilda wears a blouse with puffed sleeves and an embroidered bodice over a wide skirt.

Garland of flowers on Swanilda's romantic tutu indicates that she is a village girl

FOLK DANCE IN BALLET
Many ballets incorporate elements of folk dance. In the first act of *Coppelia,* for example, the dancers perform a stylized version of the Polish dance mazurka. Traces of other European dances, such as the Italian tarantella and the Hungarian czardas, have found their way into the ballet. This type of dancing is known as character dancing.

BUTOH EXPERIMENTAL DANCE, JAPAN
Butoh is Japan's best-known postwar experimental dance. With butoh, dancer and choreographer Tatsumi Hijikata (1928–1986) and his colleagues aimed to startle the Japanese into recognizing some of the unpleasant aspects of their society. They called their style of dancing ankoku butoh – the "dance of the dark soul." Even though butoh was a conscious attempt to break away from tradition, some elements remain rooted in classical dance. One of these elements is the very slow, stylized walk sometimes used in butoh, which can also be seen in nō.

Masklike makeup resembles the controlled faces of the dance form kabuki

Shaved heads represent a rejection of the wigs of traditional dance

Trash cans and lids provide percussion

STOMPING FORWARD IN TAP
In Britain in the late 1980s, some young dancers got together and founded a company called Tap Dogs. Rather than use conventional musical instruments as accompaniment, they explored the use of everyday and incongruous objects. The result was *Stomp*, an energetic and exhilarating work performed with great gusto.

Young men in magnificent costumes display fast and difficult footwork in the "fancy dance" contest of the powwow

Austere costumes are far removed from the elaborate kimonos of kabuki, nō, and bugaku

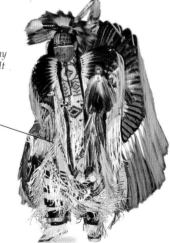

A COMMON HERITAGE
Among Native Americans, two types of dance traditions coexist. One is performed within individual tribal groups and fosters that group's identity. The other is performed by many tribal groups and fosters an overall Native American identity. Contemporary powwows (singing and dancing gatherings) feature a "fancy dance" contest.

Changes over time

THERE IS NO SINGLE HISTORY of dance; there are, rather, many histories of many dances around the world. However, all dances are rooted in the past, either because they embrace the traditions of the past, or they try to break away from them. We know of some dance traditions, such as those of ancient Greece, because the Greeks left clues in their paintings and sculptures. We know of other histories, such as how classical ballet developed, because teachers have left behind notes on steps or style. We can trace the history of Western theater dance back about 350 years, but other traditions, such as some of Japan's classical dances, go back some 1200 years! But even these dances are not unchanged relics – performers are always progressing and always innovating.

MARIE TAGLIONI
When the Italian star dancer Marie Taglioni (1804–1884) performed *La Sylphide* in 1832, she wore calf-length flowing costumes and pointe shoes to give the audience a full view of her flawless technique. Her success created such a demand for dancing on pointe that classical ballet was changed forever.

Shoes from *The Rite of Spring*

RITE OF SPRING
The Rite of Spring, a ballet about an adolescent girl dancing herself to death as a sacrifice to the god of spring, was first performed in Paris in 1913 and immediately caused a scandal. Igor Stravinsky's discordant music and Vaslav Nijinsky's groundbreaking choreography shocked an audience fed on conventional grace and beauty.

Stiff bodice was difficult to move in

Female dancers are the stars of Fokine's Les Sylphides

A 17th-century ballet costume

Longer skirt than modern costumes

LES SYLPHIDES
The popular one-act ballet *Les Sylphides* has only the barest of story lines: A poet is dazed by the presence of beautiful sylphs. With this work, first performed in 1909, the Russian choreographer Michel Fokine proved that ballet could survive and do well without being based on a complex dramatic situation.

COSTUME CHANGE
In 1760, the French choreographer Jean-Georges Noverre (1727–1810) wrote his *Lettres sur la danse et sur les ballets* (*Letters on Dancing*) as a reaction against the conventions that fettered French ballet. He appealed to dancers to take off their "enormous wigs and gigantic headdresses which destroy the true proportion of the head with the body" and to discard the "stiff and cumbersome hoops which detract from the beauties of execution."

Costumes were sumptuous with gold and silver thread on silk

RUSSIAN BALLET

ROYAL OPERA
COVENT GARDEN
· SEASON 1912 ·

SIXPENCE NET   LONDON·JOHN LONG L^{TD}

DIAGHILEV'S BALLETS RUSSES
Sergei Diaghilev's ballet company brought together the talents of the most modern dancers, designers, composers, and choreographers. From 1909 to 1929, it toured Europe and the U.S., and established ballet as a major theater art.

A modern tutu

Rhinestone decoration glistens in the stage lights

Shorter tutu allowed classical ballerinas to show off their form and technique

MARIE CAMARGO
When the Belgian dancer Marie Camargo (1710–1770) first shortened her skirt to her ankles in 1726 to show off her entrechats (jumps in which the feet cross in the air before landing), she shocked traditionalists. Men's dance costume had always been designed to allow for leaps and spins, but it was not until the 19th century that all women dancers finally began wearing a lighter, less cumbersome costume – a tutu – that allowed greater freedom of movement.

MODERN BALLET AND DANCE
By the early 20th century, ballet was seen as restrictive and rigid, so choreographers simplified costumes and invented new movements. In 1992, American dancer and choreographer Twyla Tharp restaged *Push Comes to Shove* (1976) for the Royal Ballet, with moves that were very different from the classical style.

An off-balance movement in Push Comes to Shove

Modern ballet footwork can look angular compared with classical ballet

Feet point outward with heels together

First position

Feet are spaced

Second position

Erect torso with the spine acting as the center

Third position

Legs turned out from the hips, so body is open toward the front

Fourth position

Curved arms, held en haut, or high up

Fifth position

CENTURIES OF TRADITION AND TECHNIQUE
All dance traditions are grounded in technique. Dancers go through a progression of movements and exercises that create the ideal physique for each style. Ballet, for example, is based on five classical positions devised by Pierre Beauchamp (c.1631–1705) around 1700. The five positions lay down basic rules for ballet.

Groups and shapes

Sometimes the relationship between dancers produces patterns that create specific dance formations. Group dances can be divided into two types. In the first, dancers keep their places within the formation throughout the dance: whether the dancers move in a circle, in straight lines, in figure eights, or in spirals, they remain in line and are led by the dance leader. In the second type, dancers change places through movements including chains, crossings, bridges, or stars. They dance independently within a dance, but interact with other dancers at different times. Each dancer usually ends up back in his or her starting position.

KOREAN FAN DANCERS
Dancers can carry props to create beautiful and colorful shapes in the air. For example, some traditional Korean dancers use large fans to extend their movements. Grouped together, the shapes and movements of the fan dancers create a stunning spectacle.

SQUARE DANCING
Modern square dancing is largely derived from a 19th-century European dance known as the quadrille, where four couples danced in a square formation. In the modern square dance, couples may change partners, or exchange places, or take turns dancing alone. The figures can be quite complex, and a caller shouts out instructions.

In many dances, male dancers hold each other's hands or a handkerchief

The dance leader often performs his own improvised steps

The traditional skirt is known as a foustanella

GREEK DANCING
Many dances in Greece are performed in open circles: the dancers form a chain, holding each other by the hands, waists, or shoulders and move in a circle. The first and last positions are clearly distinguished. The leader can take the chain wherever he or she wants. The order taken by the dancers usually reflects seniority. Commonly, men are at the beginning of a chain in descending order of age, followed by women, also ranked according to age.

In Hindu mythology, the gods create the universe by dancing in a magnificent circular formation, kicking away the dust of chaos as they go

IN THE ROUND
The circle is a very common dance formation. It can move either clockwise or counterclockwise. Any central figures in a circle may have special significance. Most often the dancers in a circle are on equal terms with one another – everyone can see everyone else – and they usually have to move in unison.

Krishna is often represented as a heavenly dancer

FORMATIONS IN MUSICALS
American musicals developed the Eastern European folk tradition of the double story, in which dancers of one circle stand or sit on the shoulders of another circle. The musicals of the 1920s and 1930s achieved stunning visual effects based on the multiple story.

Flower detail on muslin cloth echoes the pattern of the dance

MAYPOLES AROUND THE WORLD
The center of a circle is the focus of a circular dance. Maypole dances, in which participants dance around a long pole, exist everywhere. The pole often symbolizes fertility.

Bolivian tape dance

Ribbons held by the dancer are twisted attractively one over another in the course of the dance

An 18th-century embroidered muslin cloth showing Krishna dancing with the gopis (cowherds), North India

47

Dance and community

WHETHER WE ARE watching or participating, dance is a way of uniting communities and is commonly linked to leisure, sport, and competition. Ballroom dancing is now one of the most popular recreations in the U.S. and Europe. Its beauty and romance allow both the dancers and the audience to escape reality. Meanwhile, in dance halls throughout the world, young people meet and let off steam on the dance floor. Carnivals – including the spectacular annual events of Rio de Janeiro and New Orleans – provide ample opportunity for entertainment and merrymaking, and in many areas folk dances preserve the traditions of the past while giving a sense of well-being to the participants.

Female dancers wear exquisite gowns, often embroidered with rhinestones

Partners make imperceptible signals with their index fingers to indicate changes in rhythm or steps

For some dances, such as the waltz, male dancers dress formally in white tie and tails

BALLROOM DANCING
Throughout the U.S. and Europe, thousands of people attend ballroom-dancing classes in order to learn the skills necessary to attend dances and enter competitions. Ballroom dancing was popularized by Irene and Vernon Castle in the U.S. in the 1910s. Today, fans of dances such as the waltz, fox trot, cha-cha, and quickstep feel that this sophisticated style of dancing, with its beautiful costumes and melodic accompaniment, is reminiscent of an earlier, more elegant time.

Feathers enhance the dancer's graceful movements

ORIGINS OF BALLROOM DANCE
Contemporary ballroom dancing grew out of several traditions. Regional dances performed by the common people were the basis for many of these dances. In the 16th century, traveling dance masters began teaching both "city" and "country" styles of dance, and the two styles influenced each other. By the 19th century, aristocratic gatherings such as the ball depicted above, also contributed to the tradition. By the 20th century this style of dance was further enriched by the inclusion of African influences.

CARNIVAL
Both in Europe and in the Americas, carnivals have allowed people to dance in the streets and generally turn the social order upside down. For this reason, the authorities have often frowned upon carnival merrymaking

FOLK DANCE
The Industrial Revolution in Europe inspired nostalgia for an idealized golden past – a time when peasants enjoyed traditional country pursuits. This interest in the life of the common country people widened to include dance, and in 1893 a Folk Dance Society was set up in Stockholm, Sweden. Many more such societies followed in other parts of Europe in an attempt to rescue vanishing folk cultures.

Swedish folk dancers in traditional dress

1992 Winter Olympic Games opening ceremony, Albertville, France

Bold movements and vivid costumes could be seen from a distance

DANCE AND CEREMONY
Throughout history, as rituals and ceremonies became meaningless or were lost, they were replaced by new ones. In modern times, sport is one of the last remaining – and most important – pursuits that people enjoy together. Pageantry and ritual surround major sporting events. The Winter Olympic Games are watched by people all over the world. The spectacular opening and closing ceremonies are always marked by presentational dance and pageant.

Paris dance hall, late 19th century

EARLY DANCE HALLS
Ordinary people were generally excluded from the elegant balls held by the aristocracy. By the late 18th century, they began to establish public dance halls of their own for the enjoyment of dancing. By the 1890s, people in large cities were flocking to halls, such as the one shown here to dance and have a good time.

Sets for dance

Dance can be performed in all sorts of surroundings, from the most elaborate theater stage to a clearing in the bush. The place where the dance is performed is known as the set. A set has a great influence on the relationship between dancers and audience. Its appearance is dictated by the location and the type of dance – for example, a processional street dance must have a mobile set, if it has one at all. Western theaters tend to have more lavish sets, while Asian theaters (with the exception of the complex sets often used for Japanese kabuki) tend to have fixed, plain backgrounds. If there is no set, performers must bring a story to life by means of their bodies alone, making the audience "see" the voyages, hunts, or battles taking place.

DANCING IN THE STREET
Street parades, such as this festival in Japan, invite a community to take over public spaces and celebrate in dance. Open-air dance is more appropriate to audience participation than theater performances.

SET DESIGN FOR *SWAN LAKE,* **1989**
Set is all-important in establishing the mood of a ballet. This model is for the ballroom in Act III of *Swan Lake,* one of the most famous and popular classical ballets of all time. With its score by the 19th-century Russian composer Peter Ilyich Tchaikovsky, the set was designed to evoke a regal atmosphere by placing *Swan Lake* in the court of the Russian czar. The set features fantasy elements combined with accurate historical details. The jewels, heavy loops of gold, and imperial purple drapes all convey the magnificence of the czar's palaces.

Original sketch for the 1943 set

UPDATING SET DESIGNS FOR *SWAN LAKE,* **1943**
The British Royal Ballet performed *Swan Lake* to audiences of thousands against a set that was first designed in 1943. The old set and costumes were updated in 1989, giving a different look to one of the world's favorite ballets and creating a different atmosphere for new generations of ballet-goers. The production, costumes, and sets were all transformed by designer Yolande Sonnabend.

Set model for production of *Swan Lake* at the Royal Opera House, London, 1989

SWAN LAKE, ACT III

The ballroom scene, shown here, is at the center of *Swan Lake*. During the ball, Prince Siegfried is deceived into proposing marriage to Odile, the daughter of the evil conjuror, Rothbart. Rothbart watches gleefully as the pair dance a glorious pas de deux.

The queen's throne

Ladies-in-waiting

The evil conjuror Rothbart

Prince Siegfried's mother, the queen

GOING TO A DISCO

Discotheques – nightclubs where people dance primarily to recorded music (rather than live) – were introduced in the 1950s but were most popular in the late 1970s and 1980s. Large clubs were filled with crowds, and featured lasers and light shows to create a fantastic environment. Record companies helped discos become more popular by releasing disco singles and generating big money for the entertainment industry.

Ornamental details evoke a sense of fantasy

Bejeweled set inspired by the Russian court jeweler, Fabergé

Queen's throne

Sketch looks menacing

Puttin' on the Ritz, set design, 1929

Movements make the actual set less menacing

Puttin' on the Ritz, actual set, 1929

DANCE SETS AND HOLLYWOOD

Some of the most amazing dance sets ever seen were created for Hollywood musicals such as *Puttin' on the Ritz* by Busby Berkeley (1895–1976). Having introduced sound to the movies in 1927, producers fed the cinema-going public song-and-dance extravaganzas as a vehicle for the new technology. The spectacular sets successfully held the audience's attention despite sometimes weak plots and scripts! Berkeley was a master at lavish musicals – even today, the dance settings in his movies seem fantastically imaginative.

Behind the scenes

WHEN WE THINK ABOUT theater dance we think first of dancers, then of choreographers, then – possibly – of composers, musicians, and designers. Many more people, however, are involved behind the scenes in dance productions. Dance is full of nondancers: notators who write down steps and restage works; lighting designers who transform moods and enrich the sets; teachers and therapists who keep dancers' bodies finely tuned; people who look after shoes, costumes, and wigs; sound technicians, stagehands, painters, carpenters, box office personnel, front office managers, public relations people, administrators, critics . . . the list is endless! Most of these people never make a dance movement or are even seen by an audience. Nonetheless, they are an integral part of dance, and no performance can take place without their input. Dance productions are a cooperative venture, both on and off the stage.

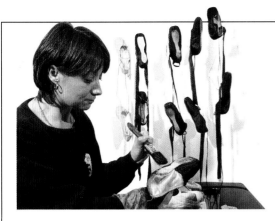

SHOE MISTRESS OR MASTER
Dancers often wear special shoes, such as pointe shoes, which are specifically designed for their type of dancing. A shoe mistress or master needs to look after the shoes, making sure that they are in good condition, that they are the right color for the costumes, and that they are replaced when necessary.

Scale model for The Nutcracker

STAGE SETS
To create the set – the scenery on the stage – the designer discusses the overall vision with the choreographer before designing the set on paper. When these ideas are approved, an accurate scale model is usually built to see if the design works in three dimensions. When built, the design may be altered until the artistic director feels it is just right.

Painting the set for
Alice in Wonderland,
1995

Massive flowers give a fanciful, fairy-tale impression

Paints and paintbrush

Lighting rig

LIGHTING
Stage lights can create a huge variety of moods and impressions, and enhance the theater sets and dance costumes. In the ballet *Petrushka*, for example, blue lights are used to give the cold feeling of a Russian winter. Lights hung above the stage and in the auditorium are referred to as the rig. The rig is controlled electronically from a central box.

PAINTERS AND CARPENTERS
Once the sets are designed, they have to be made to create the impression presented on paper. Background scenes may be painted onto backdrops. Alternatively, they may be built out of wood, with windows and doors through which dancers can enter and leave the stage. The sets need to be maintained as they are moved in and out of the theater and taken on tour.

Small scissors are used to cut thread

WARMING UP

Prior to a performance, dancers need to warm up onstage at a portable barre brought in by stagehands. They may start with pliés or knee bends, or they may have their own exercise routines. The warm-up gradually builds up include strenuous exercises involving the feet, ankles, and knees. Good warm-up is crucial to dancers to prevent them from injuring their muscles. Dancers wear a variety of casual, comfortable clothing to keep them warm before getting into their costumes.

Pins are used to hold fabric together before sewing

A pair of small needlework scissors and pins

A dressmaker in her studio

MAKING COSTUMES

Costume designers make detailed sketches of their ideas and often attach samples of possible fabrics. These are given to skilled dressmakers and tailors who then turn the designs into costumes. Costumes must never restrict movements. Sleeves must allow the arms to move freely, and fastenings must be comfortable for the dancer, but also allow for quick changes. Costumiers, as they are sometimes called, can become close to the dancers they dress. Anna Pavlova's personal dresser, Manya Charchevenikova, stayed with the great dancer until her death, becoming an intimate and privileged friend.

Makeup brushes and lipstick

MAKING UP

Makeup is used to accentuate a dancer's features. It must be quite vivid and applied heavily so that dancers' faces can be seen under strong stage lighting. Different makeup can create different expressions, such as mournfulness or fierceness. Sometimes it can completely change the shape of a dancer's face, especially if "putty" is used to make a false nose or chin. Makeup for beautiful characters, such as the Sugar Plum Fairy in *The Nutcracker*, concentrates on eyes and lips.

Specially lit mirror is needed to ensure that makeup can be seen under lights

Warming up at a portable barre

Making up for *The Nutcracker*

Famous dancers

A DANCE EXISTS ONLY while it is being performed – and yet sometimes a performance can leave an impression so strong that it stays in the memory forever. Some dancers dazzle audiences with their technical skills and physical prowess, while others stir us emotionally, through their special ability to interpret a story. Few dancers are capable of both in equal measure, but those who are often become so famous that their names go down in history. In fact, dance history is largely the history of the most famous dancers – unique performers and teachers who devoted their lives to dance, such as Anna Pavlova, Vaslav Nijinsky, and Rukmini Devi. In the eyes of the world, their names are legendary and have come to symbolize the dance they loved so much.

Pavlova's main talent lay in her expressive movements

RUKMINI DEVI
Inspired by Anna Pavlova, Rukmini Devi (1904–1986) dedicated her life to the revival of classical dance in her native India, enchanting audiences by her performances.

KATHERINE DUNHAM
An exceptionally skilled and admired dancer, choreographer, and scholar, Katherine Dunham (born 1910) created a completely original dance technique in the late 1930s. She combined ballet with movements from African and Caribbean dance traditions.
Dunham is often seen as a major figure in African-American dance, but in fact her pioneering technique is very much part of mainstream modern dance.

Dunham founded her own dance school in 1945

Pavlova as a bacchante (a dancing girl from Greek mythology)

Rogers and Astaire in *Roberta* (1935)

ANNA PAVLOVA
To the thousands who saw her perform – and the millions who know her name – the Russian ballerina Anna Pavlova (1881–1931) was the essence of ballet. An outstandingly expressive performer, she was famous for her ability to interpret a story. Pavlova once said that she wanted to "dance for everybody in the world," and she toured constantly. From 1910 to 1925, she visited Europe, the Americas, Asia, and South Africa, performing nearly 4,000 times and inspiring many dancers and choreographers.

FRED ASTAIRE AND GINGER ROGERS
A film producer once told dancer Fred Astaire (1899–1987) that he could only "dance a little." Astaire, with dance partner Ginger Rogers (1911–1995), later became an international star. Gracefully anticipating each other's smallest movements, the pair expressed perfectly the romance of ballroom dancing.

*Nijinsky in his
costume as a
faun, for the
ballet L'Après-
midi d'un faune*

Martha Graham
in *Salem Shore*
(1941)

MARTHA GRAHAM
To most people, breathing is a mundane fact of
life. To dancer Martha Graham (1894–1991), it was
a fascinating process. From her observations of
breathing, she developed the principles of
"contraction and release," on which she based
her pioneering style of modern dance.

JORGE DONN
Born in Argentina, ballet dancer Jorge
Donn (1947–1992) was famous for his
powers of interpretation. His flawless
technique enabled him to use his whole
body to communicate with an audience.

VASLAV NIJINSKY
Russian dance legend Vaslav Nijinsky
(1890–1950) is best remembered
for his remarkable jumps, or
elevations. In the 1911 ballet *Le
Spectre de la Rose*, in which he
portrayed the spirit of a rose,
he soared out of a window
into the night, creating
probably the most
famous leap in ballet
history. Nijinsky was
also famous for
his controversial
choreographies, such
as *L'Après-midi d'un
faune* (1912). On its opening
night, members of the audience
alleged that this ballet was obscene,
and fights broke out.

*Nijinsky's mystical
costume was created
by Russian designer
Léon Bakst*

55

Choreography

THE WORD *CHOREOGRAPHY* comes from the Greek *graphia*, meaning "to write down," and *choros*, meaning "dance." Today, choreography refers more to the invention of dances than to the mere writing down of dance steps, and a choreographer is an inventor of a new sequence of dance steps. The importance of the choreographer varies from one society to another. In Japan, some classical dances have been choreographed and are performed only by specific families. In many African and European folk dances, some dance steps are remembered and handed down through generations – they may be named after their choreographers. In Western theater dance like ballet, choreography is a profession and choreographers can become world-famous.

Perrot with Carlotta Grisi, for whom he choreographed *Giselle* (1841)

JULES PERROT
During his lifetime, Jules Perrot (1810–1894) created expressive choreography that helped tell the story of his ballets through movement. His convincing characters came from all social classes, but his heroes were frequently of humble origins.

MARIE RAMBERT
Trained in a method of rhythmic analysis known as eurythmics, Polish-born Marie Rambert (1888–1982) studied in Paris. While there, she was hired by Sergei Diaghilev of the Ballets Russes to help dancers with the complex score of *The Rite of Spring*. In 1931, she established Britain's first permanent ballet company and school in London, and nurtured the talents of famous choreographers, including Frederick Ashton.

Lean, long-legged dancers were ideal for Balanchine's type of work

GEORGE BALANCHINE
The name of George Balanchine (1904–1983) is synonymous with American classical ballet. Originally from Russia, Balanchine emigrated to the U.S. and set up the School of American Ballet in 1934, planting the seed for the future New York City Ballet (1948). Balanchine's swift, athletic style came to be seen as distinctively American.

Balanchine (center) demonstrating a pas de deux position, 1950

MERCE CUNNINGHAM
After working with Martha Graham, the American dancer Merce Cunningham (born 1919) developed his own original style. Although he worked out his dance movements in some detail, their order was left up to the performers – or even determined by flipping a coin! In his choreographies, he gives equal importance to each area of the stage and sees sound, decor, and movement as independent entities.

The position of this dancer is recorded in Benesh movement notation (BMN), below right

Hands are held above the head

In BMN, five horizontal lines represent the level of the head, shoulders, waist, knees, and floor

Elbows and knees are indicated by crossing basic signs

	Head
	Shoulder
	Waist
	Knees

Floor

BENESH MOVEMENT NOTATION
Benesh movement notation, or BMN, was developed in England in the 1940s by Rudolf and Joan Benesh. It is a movement – rather than dance – notation, and can record what the body does in any activity, whether it is ballet or football. Today many dance companies employ Benesh notators to write down scores of the choreographies in their repertoire.

des Vaißeaux   41

Musical score is included to ensure that music and steps complement each other

Step symbols are placed beside a central line

Right and left are shown by placement of symbols on either side of the central line

Feuillet's notation system

Central line shows the floor pattern of the dance

NOTATION SYSTEM
In 1701, a French dancing master, Raoul Feuillet (c.1675–c.1730), wrote his *Chorégraphie ou l'art d'écrire la danse (Choreography or the Art of Writing Dance)*, giving a notation system for writing down basic movements, rather than the conventional steps that everyone knew. The system quickly became accepted by dance masters throughout Europe. It allowed them to recreate each other's choreographies with a minimum of effort.

Left hand is in front of the body with palm facing front

Right foot is raised to waist level behind the body

Right arm is raised to shoulder level behind the body

Left foot is on pointe

Position of body in BMN as seen from the dancer's point of view

ARABESQUE IN BMN
This arabesque is notated as a static picture. A full score would indicate how the dancer moves into and out of the position as well as her timing. The left arm is raised in front of the body (vertical dash) above the head, the right arm is behind (a dot) at shoulder level. The left foot is on pointe, level with the body (horizontal dash), while the right foot is raised behind the body.

Dance crazes

DANCING IS A PART of every society's culture – and a dance craze can test a society's tolerance levels. The history of dance in Europe and the U.S. shows how some dances that today represent elegance and sophistication were once thought deeply shocking. For example, polite society was appalled when the waltz was introduced because for the first time men and women danced in a close embrace instead of at arm's length. Some dances were deemed so outrageous that they were outlawed. In the 1910s, one woman spent 50 days in jail for dancing a banned dance called the turkey trot! Despite such reactions, fashionable people through the ages have wanted to learn the latest crazes.

SHOCKING WALTZ
In the 1780s, the waltz gripped Germany. At first people frowned upon the abandonment of the whirling couples and claimed that the dance was weakening the bodies and minds of the younger generation.

DOING THE CAKEWALK
The cakewalk was a craze of the 1890s. The dance originated on sugarcane plantations, where, after harvest, plantation owners would set up a dance competition for their enslaved African workers. The slaves who made up the fanciest dance steps won cakes. The cakewalk, with its strutlike steps, broke the tradition of smooth, gliding dances that had been dominant in the past.

A strutting style is characteristic of cakewalking

CHARLESTON
In the 1920s, the charleston conquered New York. Its origins dated back to World War I, when many African-Americans left the poverty of the southern states to work in New York's munitions factories. They brought with them a high-stepping dance style, which was featured in popular African-American musicals, such as *Runnin' Wild*. From the shows, the craze spread all over the city and to all sections of society.

Sometimes dancers knocked hats off the heads of their audience with their spectacular high kicks

Toulouse-Lautrec's "Moulin Rouge"

Cancan dancers lifted and swirled the fronts of their dresses

The cancan's finale eventually featured splits

CANCAN AT THE MOULIN ROUGE
In the 1830s, the cancan, featuring a line of high-kicking women, hit Parisian ballrooms. As the cancan became more wild and acrobatic, it was seen by many as immoral. By the 1880s, the cancan had moved into music halls, such as the Moulin Rouge. The French artist Henri de Toulouse-Lautrec (1864–1901) immortalized the dance in his posters.

ROCK 'N' ROLL DANCERS
In the 1950s, rock 'n' roll music and dance were all the rage. Couples moved exuberantly around the dance floor, reinventing old steps from the charleston and the lindy hop (a fast, improvised 1930s dance). Partners showed off to friends with acrobatic moves such as "air steps," in which the man spun his partner through the air.

In rock 'n' roll dancing, the man leads his partner through different moves

Chubby Checker, who had a hit single called "The Twist"

The leading dancer always holds his partner's right hand with his own left hand

Dancers try to make even difficult moves look effortless

LET'S TWIST AGAIN
The twist caught on in the 1960s. It brought a development as revolutionary as the first closed-couple waltz – partners let go of each other! They stepped apart to wriggle and shake on their own. No one led, no one followed, no one even needed to know the steps!

Light-up heels

Adapter for recharging batteries in shoes

discoshoes

DISCO MANIA
Dancers have always invented dramatic outfits: red boots for tango, beaded fringed dresses for the charleston – even sandals with flashing lights for disco. These "disco shoes," complete with batteries, became fashionable after the movie *Saturday Night Fever* was released in 1977, and disco became the hottest dance craze of its time.

Index

Acknowledgments

Dorling Kindersley would like to thank:
Mary Shanley; Kalamandalam Vijayakumar at Kala Chethena Kathakali Troupe; Graham Mitchell and the Adonais Ballet Company; Indonesian Embassy and Gillian Roberts; Freed of London Ltd., for supply of ballet shoes; Anusha Subramanyam and Vipul Sangoi; Eric Pierrat at Gallimard Editions.

Editorial and research assistants: Joanne Matthews, Katie Martin, Robert Graham

Design assistants: Goldy Broad, Maggie Tingle, Venice Shone, Elizabeth Nicola

Additional photography: Susanna Price, Gary Ombler

Picture credits
The publisher would like to thank the following for their kind permission to reproduce the images:

(t = top, b = bottom, c = center, l = left, r = right)

AKG London: 30tl (insert); Erich Lessing/Musee de Louvre, Paris 37bl.
Axiom: Jim Holmes 10tl.
Patrick Baldwin: 52tl, 52bl, 52cl, 53tr, 53bl, 53br.
Bata Shoe Museum, Canada: 24tr, 25tc, 59cr.
Dominique Bernard: 19tl.
Bibliothèque Nationale de France, Paris: 29tr, 57cl.
Bridgeman Art Library, London/New York: Detail inside a Kylix from Vulci c. 520–510 BC British Museum, London 9br; *Buffalo Dance* by George Catlin (1794–1872) Location Unknown 18c; *The Dancing Class*, c.1873-76 by Edgar Degas (1834–1917) Musée d'Orsay, Paris, France 13tr; *Pavlova as a Bacchante* by Sir John Lavery (1856–1941) Glasgow Art Gallery and Museum 54tr; *Poster for the Moulin Rouge*, 1891 by Henri de Toulouse-Lautrec (1864–1901) Victoria & Albert Museum, London 58br.
Britstock-IFA: F Aberham 36r.
Carroll & Brown: 48c.
Christie's Images: Angels & Bermans 30tl, Royal Opera House 31tr, *A Ballroom Scene* by Victor Gabriel Gilbert (1847–1935) 49tl.
Commonwealth Institute: 29cl.
Dee Conway: 9tr, 20bl, 21br, 28bc, 39tr, Kirov Ballet 20tr, The Georgian State Dance Company 29c, Adventures in Motion Pictures 41bl, Royal Festival Hall 43tr, Royal Ballet 33bc, 41tl, 45cr, Merce Cunningham Dance Company 57tl.

Bill Cooper: Birmingham Royal Ballet 17cl.
Corbis UK Ltd.: Bettmann/UPI 56bl; Robbie Jack 44bl.
Dominic Photography: Catherine Ashmore 42br.
Dover Publications, Inc.: *Great Ballet Prints of the Romantic Era*, Parmenia Migel, 1981 44tl.
Enguerand-Iliade: Agnès Courrault 41r; Colette Masson 28bl, 40tr, 43cl, 55cr.
Robert Estall Photo Agency: Carol Beckwith 26bl.
E.T. Archive: 51br, 51cr; Royal Ballet Benevolent Fund 50bl; Victoria & Albert Museum 55l, *Carlotta Grisi & Jules Perot in La Polka* by J Bouvier, 1844 56tr.
Mary Evans Picture Library: 8c (above), 12l, 37r, 42bl, 49br, 58cl, 58bl, 58tl.
Exeter City Museums and Art Gallery, Royal Albert Memorial Museum: 4cl, 35cr.
Eye Ubiquitous: David Cumming 19b; Matthew McKee 18br.
Glasgow Museums: St. Mungo Museum of Religious Life and Art 35c.
The Granger Collection, New York: 58tr.
Ronald Grant Archive: 47tr.
The Horniman Museum, London: 4tl, 4bc, 6tl, 6tl (insert), 6cl, 9bc, 15tc, 15c, 15tcr, 15tr, 15cr, 15crr, 20tl, 32tr, 32c, 32bl, 33cr, 36c.
Hulton Getty: 18bl, 35br, 55tr, 59l, 59tr.
Hutchison Library: 8tr; Andre Singer 27br; Anna Tully 37tl; COJ Hatt 38br.
Image Bank: A. Boccaccio 49tc; David W. Hamilton 39bl; Frans Lemmens 32br; Nicolas Russell 51tl; Steve Niedorf 52cr (below).
Images Color Library: 22cl, 26c.
Images of Africa Photobank: David Keith Jones 25tr, 39br.
Kobal Collection: MGM, 1952 8bl; RKO 54br.

Macquitty International Photo Collection: 14cl.
Novosti: 23tr.
Panos Pictures: Penny Tweedie 16tr.
Performing Arts Library: 54tl, 54bl, 56cr; Ben Christopher 10bl; Clive Barda 26cl, 40bl; Emily Booth 17tl; Jane Mont 46tl; Marcelo Benoahan 12cr, 28br; Michael Diamond 45tl.
Pictor International: 11bl, 11tl, 16bl, 38l, 43br, 46bl, 47br.
The Royal Ballet School: 12 tr, 12 tl, 12 bc, 12 br, 13 bl, 13 cl, 13 cr, 13 br, 13 tc.
Sotheby's Transparency Library: The Dressing Room by Dame Laura Knight 1877–1970 © Dame Laura Knight, reproduced by permission of Curtis Brown Ltd., London 26bc.
South American Pictures: Robert Francis 39tl; Sue Mann 14c; Tony Morrison 10cr.
Frank Spooner Pictures: Eric Brissaud/Gamma 36bl; Jo Pool /Gamma Press 49c.
Tony Stone Images: Bruno de Hogues 14/15b; Chad Ehlers 49tr; Christopher Arnesen 32cl; David Hiser 32tl; Gerard Pile 34cl; Hugh Sitton 11r; Marcus Brooke 23cl; Penny Tweedie 34bl; Phil Schermeister 46cl; Rex A. Butcher 50tl.
Angela Taylor: Royal Ballet 51tr.
Telegraph Colour Library: 17r.
V & A Picture Library: 16br, 28tr, 44tr, 47c, 50/51b.
Wallace Collection: 37cl (above), 37tl (below), 37cl.

Jacket:
The Bata Shoe Museum, Canada: Front tr; **Christie's Images:** Back tl; **Mary Evans Picture Library:** Front br, Back cl; **The Horniman Museum, London:** Front cl, cr, br; **Hulton Getty:** Back br; **Novosti:** Front cl (above); **Telegraph Colour Library:** Front cr (below).

DK EYEWITNESS BOOKS

SUBJECTS

HISTORY

AFRICA

ANCIENT CHINA

ARMS & ARMOR

BATTLE

CASTLE

COWBOY

EXPLORER

KNIGHT

MEDIEVAL LIFE

MYTHOLOGY

NORTH AMERICAN INDIAN

PIRATE

PRESIDENTS

RUSSIA

SHIPWRECK

TITANIC

VIKING

WITCHES & MAGIC-MAKERS

ANCIENT WORLDS

ANCIENT EGYPT

ANCIENT GREECE

ANCIENT ROME

AZTEC, INCA & MAYA

BIBLE LANDS

MUMMY

PYRAMID

THE BEGINNINGS OF LIFE

ARCHEOLOGY

DINOSAUR

EARLY HUMANS

PREHISTORIC LIFE

THE ARTS

BOOK

COSTUME

DANCE

FILM

MUSIC

TECHNOLOGY

BOAT

CAR

FLYING MACHINE

FUTURE

INVENTION

SPACE EXPLORATION

TRAIN

PAINTING

GOYA

IMPRESSIONISM

LEONARDO & HIS TIMES

MANET

MONET

PERSPECTIVE

RENAISSANCE

VAN GOGH

WATERCOLOR

SCIENCE

ASTRONOMY

CHEMISTRY

EARTH

ECOLOGY

ELECTRICITY

ELECTRONICS

ENERGY

EVOLUTION

FORCE & MOTION

HUMAN BODY

LIFE

LIGHT

MATTER

MEDICINE

SKELETON

TECHNOLOGY

TIME & SPACE

SPORT

BASEBALL

FOOTBALL

OLYMPICS

SOCCER

SPORTS

ANIMALS

AMPHIBIAN

BIRD

BUTTERFLY & MOTH

CAT

DOG

EAGLE &
BIRDS OF PREY

ELEPHANT

FISH

GORILLA,
MONKEY & APE

HORSE

INSECT

MAMMAL

REPTILE

SHARK

WHALE

HABITATS

ARCTIC & ANTARCTIC

DESERT

JUNGLE

OCEAN

POND & RIVER

SEASHORE

THE EARTH

CRYSTAL & GEM

FOSSIL

HURRICANE &
TORNADO

PLANT

ROCKS & MINERALS

SHELL

TREE

VOLCANO &
EARTHQUAKE

WEATHER

THE WORLD AROUND US

BUILDING

CRIME & DETECTION

FARM

FLAG

MEDIA &
COMMUNICATIONS

MONEY

RELIGION

SPY

Future updates and editions will be available online at www.dk.com

A–Z

DK EYEWITNESS BOOKS

1–110

Future updates and editions will be available online at www.dk.com

DORLING KINDERSLEY EYEWITNESS BOOKS

1. BIRD
2. ROCKS & MINERALS
3. SKELETON
4. ARMS & ARMOR
5. TREE
6. POND & RIVER
7. BUTTERFLY & MOTH
8. SPORTS
9. SHELL
10. EARLY HUMANS
11. MAMMAL
12. MUSIC
13. DINOSAUR
14. PLANT
15. SEASHORE
16. FLAG
17. INSECT
18. MONEY
19. FOSSIL
20. FISH
21. CAR
22. FLYING MACHINE
23. ANCIENT EGYPT
24. ANCIENT ROME
25. CRYSTAL & GEM
26. REPTILE
27. INVENTION
28. WEATHER
29. CAT
30. BIBLE LANDS
31. EXPLORER
32. DOG
33. HORSE
34. FILM
35. COSTUME
36. BOAT
37. ANCIENT GREECE
38. VOLCANO & EARTHQUAKE
39. TRAIN
40. SHARK
41. AMPHIBIAN
42. ELEPHANT
43. KNIGHT
44. MUMMY
45. COWBOY
46. WHALE
47. AZTEC, INCA & MAYA
48. BOOK
49. CASTLE
50. VIKING
51. DESERT
52. PREHISTORIC LIFE
53. PYRAMID
54. JUNGLE
55. ANCIENT CHINA